PR[illegible] TRAVELLER

By the same author:
My friend Arnold's Book of Personal Computers

THE PRACTICAL TRAVELLER

Gareth Powell

ALLEN & UNWIN

For Meurig - the first great traveller

First published in 1990
Allen & Unwin Australia Pty Ltd
8 Napier Street, North Sydney, NSW 2059 Australia

National Library of Australia
Cataloguing-in-publication entry:
Powell, Gareth.
The practical traveller.

Includes index.
ISBN 0 04 300106 8.

1. Voyages and travels - Guide-books. I. Title
910.202

Set in 10/11 pt Palatino by Gareth Powell Pty Ltd
Printed by Southwood Press, Marrickville, NSW Australia

Contents

Introduction

I am passionate about travel, but I am no lover of the colourful school of travel writing. Phrases that tell of golden beaches, dramatic sunsets, crossroads of the Orient, places where East meets West leave me unmoved. What I prefer is straight, genuine, useful fact, amusingly written. And the occasional drop of acid.

This book gives advice to travellers. Real advice based on real experience. It also has, I hope, the odd humorous moment built in. Part of this book appeared originally in *The Sydney Morning Herald*, a newspaper of which I am travel editor. However, all the articles have been updated and, in many cases, considerably extended. About half the book is totally new material.

In reading this book you should accept an element of bias. I love travel. I travel more than most people. I have travelled, since 1950, more than most people. More times around the world then I care to remember. Always with joy and hope in my heart. There are some areas I am fairly weak on—specifically the middle of Africa. And I have a bias towards travelling cheaply on a tight budget. Luxurious hotels attract me not. First class is terra incognita. No luxury cruise ship has ever had me as a passenger.

These are the omissions. The bias is because I see travel through a pair of rose tinted spectacles but with slightly cynical eyes.

Not everyone, all gods be praised, loves travel, people, places as I do.

Regard S. J. Perelman, the American humorist, on the subject of Georgetown in Penang, 'Of all the lethargic, benighted, somnolent fleabags this side of Hollywood, the port of Georgetown on the island of Penang is the most abysmal'. He wrote this in a strange work entitled *Westward Ha!* which might possibly be indicative of his state of mind. I had lunch with him in Hong Kong just before he did his last trip into China in an elderly MG. He had not changed his opinion in the slightest. He was also pretty scathing about the rest of Asia. Perelman was not, I believe, a romantic traveller.

Russia has been vilified by almost everyone. Matthew Arnold, back in 1885, wrote of it as 'the country where one would least like to live'.

Knocking Russia is easy. but what about Tahiti, that paradise on earth? And Papeete, its capital? D.H. Lawrence wrote of it in 1922, 'Papeete is a poor sort of a place, mostly Chinese, natives in European clothes, and fat. These are supposed to be the earthly paradises: these South Sea Isles. You can have' em'.

Nor was Evelyn Waugh a writer who loved paradise, 'General impression of Trinidad is that I don't want to see it again".

In roughly the same area, Aldous Huxley did not go into raptures about Belize when it was British Honduras. He wrote in 1934, in *Beyond Mexique Bay*,'If the world had any ends, British Honduras would certainly be one of them'.

The West Indies has always attracted the censure of writers. In 1859, Anthony Trollope wrote, in *The West Indies and the Spanish Main*, 'It is one of the few sores on our huge and healthy carcass; and the sore has been now running so long, that we have almost given over asking whether it is curable'.

Very few places escape the travel writers' wrath. Buenos Aires was described in 1827 by Captain F.B. Head in *Rough notes across the Pampas and the Andes* as 'far from being an agreeable residence for those who are accustomed to English comfort'. He went on to explain why. 'The water is extremely impure, scarce and expensive. The towns badly paved and dirty, and the houses the most uncomfortable abodes I have ever entered'.

Elsewhere in South America, the new city of Brasilia did not meet with unalloyed approval. Arthur Schlesinger wrote of it in *One Thousand Days*, as follows, 'We drove through the impersonal and sinister streets of Brasilia, the terrifying preview of a collectivist future'.

R.B. Cunninghame Graham, on the subject of Canada in 1898, wrote, 'Canada is said to have got its name from the two Spanish words 'Aca' and 'Nada', as signifying 'there is nothing here'.

And of Hudson's Bay, Captain James Knight, in 1717 wrote, 'I never see [sic] such a miserable place in my life'.

France, of course, is fair game for everyone. Did you recall that William Shakespeare (in *All's Well That Ends Well*) wrote, 'France is a dog-hole'. And, at a later time, Mark Twain followed with, 'France has neither winter, summer, nor morals—apart from these drawbacks, it is a fine country'.

My favourite city, Hong Kong, was described by that widely-published author, Anonymous, as 'a first-rate colony for fifth-rate Europeans'. Vicious, but true.

If all these destinations call forth such bitter comments, what of our own fair country, Australia?

Charles Darwin, in his *Journal During The Voyage Of HMS Beagle*, recorded his visit here in 1836, "I leave your shores without sorrow or regret'. D.H.Lawrence, in *Kangaroo*, thought 'the landscape is so unimpressive'. George Mikes, the Hungarian travel writer, wrote in *Boomerang*, 'There are many non-intellectual countries; Australia is one of the few anti-intellectual ones'.

However, the inveterate traveller, Alfred Viscount Northcliffe, was in disagreement, 'My impression of Australia is that there is too much amusement here. We have nothing like this at home'.

None of these was, perhaps, a romantic traveller. Perhaps they had collectively eaten something that disagreed with them. For me, travel is the last great adventure, the last great romantic adventure.

Gareth Powell
Sydney, July 1990

1

Sensible advice

Ay, now that I am in Arden: the more fool I; when I was at home, I was in a better place: but travellers must be content.

Shakespeare, *As You Like It, II, 4.*

One of the most common disrupters of marital bliss is the choice of where to spend a vacation. What this country needs is an ocean in the mountains.

Paul Sweeney

There are very few problems connected with travel around the world. Just use basic common sense and you will not get into trouble. In more than 40 years of travelling, I can count all the problems I have encountered on the fingers of two hands. And I am not a person over-endowed with common sense. Here are some basic tips which will be expanded in separate chapters later in this book:

Take care of your health. The Australian Department of Health issues a series of guidelines which, I believe, err much too far on the side of caution.

Admittedly, in my time, I must have built up a fairly spectacular collection of antibodies but I find that an intelligent approach to health serves me far better than a dozen shots. I am against most injections simply because the risk involved in having them is very frequently higher than the risk of contracting the disease.

This is my personal decision. You must decide for yourself.

Never drink the water anywhere. I have followed this rule for years, drinking instead either bottled mineral water, Coca-Cola or a bottle of the cooling amber fluid. Never take ice in your drinks unless you are in a three-star or better hotel. Freezing does not kill little buglets.

Carry your medicines with you. You may not be able to get your prescription filled precisely when you are abroad.

Take your money in a mixture of currency and travellers' cheques. The cheques should be Thomas Cook, American Express or CitiCorp. Others can create problems. The story is that if you have a travellers' cheque with a Visa symbol on it, you will have no problem changing it. I wrote this in Bangkok and the following night the hotel keeper at the Suriwongse Hotel simply didn't want to know when a German guest proffered such a cheque.

Take a credit card which is universally accepted. In some countries if you are in an accident you will not get immediate medical attention unless you are carrying a current credit card. Do not carry an American Express Gold Card, which is vulgar and marks you as a mug punter.

Read as many travel guides as you possibly can before you go. At the very least read one or two. The Lonely Planet guides, published in Melbourne, are among the best and I am also extremely impressed by the Fodor series.

Keep copies of everything. Photocopy all your documentation, including the relevant pages of your passport. This will make replacing lost documents much easier.

Hang on to your passport. Always, always, leave your passport and the major part of your money in the safe deposit of your hotel. Only carry enough cash for the day, with a little over. I always carry a screwed-up $US100 note in my pocket-book as a final emergency reserve.

Don't flash wealth. If you must go to the lower life area of town, cut right down on your drinking and leave your wallet in your hotel. Drink Coca-Cola and plead poverty. In all the bars of Asia, I am known as Cheapskate Charlie, a title of which I am inordinately proud.

See Europe off-season. Now is the winter of our discontent made glorious summer by the absence of hordes of damn tourists trampling on our feet. In the past three seasons I have come to the sad conclusion that the only possible time to see Europe is during the winter, the very early spring and the late autumn. The rest of the time the place is simply too crowded with tourists for reasonable enjoyment.

It is not that 'I do not like the human race, I do not like its dirty face'—although there is much in that— but rather that tourists, *en masse*, are something less than lovely. 'See the average tourist—How the sight appals, Spitting in Niagara Falls'.

So wrote one protester—and with a fair element of truth.

I sat with a companion in a small inn on the outskirts of Seville. Dusk was falling and a singer with a guitar was ripping his heart out for the public gaze as he told of unrequited love, wandering husbands and faithless hussies. I was sipping a gentle Carlos Primero, that most excellent of Spanish brandies.

There was a squeal of brakes outside and what was known in my youth as a charabanc drew up. It was full of English tourists led by a formidable woman whom I took to be the guide. As they passed, one earnest seeker of the truth called to her (and I promise you this is the literal truth), 'Eh, Mabel. What's Spanish for piece of cake?' This I can do without.

This summer I returned to Strasbourg cathedral to see that most glorious of Gothic monuments. In the winter the square had been busy, the inside of the cathedral easy to walk around. On an early June morning I could not, literally could not, push my way across the square. The inside of the cathedral was an unholy rugger scrum. This is not the way to view sacred architecture which was inspired by God.

I walked to see the new wonders that I.M. Pei has created at the entrance to the Louvre. There were queues to get in, queues to see *The Winged Victory*, queues to see the *Mona Lisa*, queues to go to the loo, even queues to leave. It was like wartime Britain without the good humour.

The summer has ceased to be civilised in Europe. To escape that lemming madness you must go in the chillier months. This is, of course, the problem associated with seeing Europe in the off-peak months–it is damn cold. But with the exception of Britain, especially the northerly and westerly extremes which have never learned how to cope with a severe frost, Europe has winter by the throat.

True, the chestnuts will not be in bloom in Paris. True, you may not be able to build up your tan on the beaches of Italy (but Greece, Malta, Cyprus—that's another matter). True, the Tivoli in Copenhagen, as well as many other delights, will be closed.

These are but small penalties to pay for the pleasure of being able to visit museums, theatres, art galleries, cathedrals, restaurants and all those other delights without a horde of tourists of different nationalities swarming all over you. There is little difference in the quality of tourist by nationality once assembled in groups. They are all equally loathsome. Mass tourism brings out the worst in people.

The prices are also cheaper off-season. All air travel to and around Europe is geared to the peak seasons. As are the hotel prices. Geoff Wyatt, the author, was travelling in Greece in the winter. He was staying at the Grande Bretagne, that most excellent pub in Athens. As he approached reception he took out his calculator so that he could work out the equivalent in Australian dollars of the drachmas charged for the room. He was told to put his calculator away. That week there was a standard two-thirds reduction.

In some places, this does not apply, London is one example, Brussels another. But even in these cities the hotel occupancy eases back and you may get service instead of the surly look and contempt which is the summer special.

What does one need to do to tour and travel in Europe in the winter and enjoy it as much as the summer?

Dress for the weather. The most useful garment that you can acquire for travel in the winter is a light, padded, silk Chinese jacket. I have always bought mine in Hong Kong, but I understand they are now available in Australia. These jackets are padded with shredded silk and they are warming beyond belief.

Keep your head covered. Most body heat escapes through the top of your head. I wear either a Greek sailor's cap, which I imagine makes me look rakish, or a Chinese fur hat, which I know makes me look daft. But in winter in Europe the streets are full of people looking daft and keeping warm so this is no problem.

Carry a small folding umbrella. The alleged summer in Sydney has proved the worth of these excellent contraptions.

Use the trains as far as possible. All European trains—Britain again being the exception—are warm, clean and run on time. As a way of getting from city to city, within the tight compass of that small continent, they are without parallel. Nothing is more than a day's journey away. Normally it is a question of hours and the Eurailpass becomes a wonderful bargain.

Plan well ahead. All tourist associations will be delighted to advise you of activities during the winter months. You need to make certain that what you want to see is open when you get there. This is not difficult to achieve.

Skip Scandinavia altogether unless you are a hardier soul than I. There, winter is in control. Early spring, yes. Late autumn, yes. Winter, no.

Otherwise, in winter Europe is yours. Without the tourists, without the hassle, without the bustle. I can put up with a nip in the air for these pleasures.

2

Organising yourself

Our plans miscarry because they have no aim. When a man does not know what harbour he is making for, no wind is the right wind.
Seneca

We must ask where we are and whither we are tending.
Abraham Lincoln

As a traveller I am somewhat disorganised and slightly shambolic. The only way I survive is to use a series of check lists, which I refer to before and after and during my travels to make sure I have the essentials to get me where I am going.

Checklist on the day I decide to travel

Is the flight direct?
Nothing is more irritating than to get to the airport thinking you are going directly to Hong Kong only to find you are going to Melbourne first. There you will spend a boring hour in a waiting room. This also applies on some domestic flights. Flying direct is the only way to go. Impress this on your travel agent and check it yourself, by telephone, after you have collected the tickets. Airlines, for obvious reasons, do not make much of the fact that the flight is not direct. They do not advertise it in large letters. You need to check carefully.

Watch out for anything that is called a technical stop. This is precisely the same as a normal stop in that it extends your journey by at least an hour. The airlines believe that because no passengers are getting on and off the technical stop makes little difference. Yes it does—to the passenger. An hour added to your journey on the homeward run stretches into infinity.

Can you rearrange the trip to be cheaper/more convenient/more desirable?

It is tempting to take the first itinerary or the first fare offered. It is more intelligent to think about shopping around or changing your itinerary to take advantage of reduced-fare offers. On a trip to Europe, this can save upwards of $1000.

Find out if seats on the aircraft can be booked ahead.

Do this immediately and let the carrier know about meal requests.

I am a flying vegetarian. That is, I am a serious vegetarian in the air because I believe it helps me get over travel stress more quickly. My own experience is also that vegetarian meals are fresher and better presented than normal meals. When I book, and I book as far in advance as possible, I specify vegetarian so an airline meal can be organised. Qantas has me registered as a frequent flyer and a vegetarian in its computer but it always needs to be re-confirmed on booking the flight.

Is my passport up-to-date with all the necessary visas?

I have dual nationality (Australian and British) and boast two passports. Between them, I can manage most countries without a visa, provided the passport is up-to-date and valid. Visas are essential for many countries and the airline simply will not carry you unless your passport is up-to-date and all visas in order. The airlines won't carry you because in most countries, by law, they then have to fly you back at their own expense.

If there is a commercial purpose for the travel, have I set up as many appointments in advance as possible?

An Australian business executive heads for London. Works under the assumption that appointments can be made on arrival and that the working day can be usefully filled. Hah! Getting to talk to a business executive on the telephone in Britain is difficult enough. Getting one to agree to an early appointment is almost impossible unless you are buying, they are selling.

It is true that in some countries you can wing it when setting up appointments. But not in Europe, most of Asia. Make your appointments before you travel.

Will my trip conflict with national holidays where I am going?

Trying to do business in Hong Kong during Chinese New Year is impossible. Nor during Songkran, the water festival in Thailand. If you try to set up business meetings during Wimbledon week in London, good luck to you. I do not fancy your chances. You have the same chances as setting up a meeting in Australia for Melbourne Cup Day.

Do I need any injections and do I have a sufficient supply of nostrums and medicaments to keep me healthy on the voyage?

By and large I avoid all injections as they can create more problems than they solve. If I have to have them I do it well in time. Medicines are not universally the same. In Asia, fakes exist. If you are on a prescription take enough with you. Make sure you take the prescription along as in many countries medicines are looked on as drugs and you will need supporting evidence to justify carrying them. In some countries even codeine is on the banned list.

Checklist on the day I go

Three days before I fly my list reads:

• Money. I like to carry small cash, some travellers' cheques.

- Credit cards in credit.
- Confirm bookings.
- Check suitcase is not broken and that the clothes I'll take are clean.
- Collect sufficient film for camera and check all batteries.

As I am about to leave for the airport, my partner insists I stand like a great loon holding up the appropriate objects as she goes through the list. The list includes airline tickets, passport, address book, toilet kit, medicaments (I was ever a hypochondriac), eye shades, inflatable neck support. I have different lists for different types of trips but that is the basic list.

Then at every port of call, at every check-in and check-out, I recite to myself the magic mantra 'pamcam'. It is not Sanskrit; it's an acronym for 'passport, airline tickets, money, credit cards, address book and medicines'. Providing I keep getting 'pamcam' right, I know I will probably get to my destination. For more than that the passionate traveller cannot ask.

Planning for the business traveller

Almost every business traveller has a different idea of the essentials that should be taken on an overseas or interstate trip. There is one Australian executive who swears by a supply of epoxy adhesive and another who insists on carrying a miniature microscope to inspect samples—frequently much to the distress of his suppliers.

Let us then list in order of priority the accessories which we consider almost essential for the well-equipped travelling executive.

Visiting cards

If you are travelling in Asia and you do not have a visiting card you do not exist. They are exchanged at every meeting, however casual. In Japan they are presented with both hands with a slight bowing motion as if they were a precious gift. Opinion is divided as to whether they should have your name and title in the appropriate characters in Japanese or Chinese on the back. Having seen some quite ludicrous translations, I tend to be opposed to the practice. On one aspect there is no argument. You must have a plentiful supply. Five hundred visiting cards should safely cover a three week business trip.

In some countries the title of the bearer is considered significant, in others not.

The English at the highest level, for example, go for plain cards which have been engraved and bear no business title whatsoever. It is presumed vulgar to advertise one's rank. Americans are keen on letting you know that they are Vice-Presidents. The treatment you get in certain Asian countries is directly related to the title on your card. The word 'Director' has more magic than 'Manager'. The words 'President' and 'Chairman' put you at the top of the tree. Whatever you do, do not invest in those cards which show your photograph in colour.

Portable computer
That I am biased towards personal computers is well known. My belief is that for a travelling business executive something very light and powerful is worth the extra trouble. At the moment my machine of choice is a Toshiba T1000SE but anything that weighs under 2.5 kilograms and has a backlit screen will do.

Calculator
Until quite recently one major company forbade its senior executives to use calculators, believing that it impaired their reasoning and negotiating skills. That company has now discovered that the theory does not stand up to close examination. There are two types of calculators. Those that help you through various mathematical functions to arrive at a correct and desired answer. And those that are flashy, have an improbable number of entry buttons and are covered with Greek characters which may mean much to the initiated but nothing to ordinary mortals.

The first kind is readily available and all you need is to be certain that you can get your fingers on the keys and that you can easily read the resulting answers. For this second kind of calculator some basic mathematical ability is needed. If you understand the basis of Reverse Polish Notation then you will understand how to choose and operate one.

Fluorescent underliners
A travelling executive should have a magic marker which emphasises in fluorescent yellow important points in books, letters and manuscripts. It looks extremely professional and as Doctor Johnson would say, focuses the mind wonderfully. Stabilo Boss

2 looks like a fountain pen and is refillable. There are several others on the market but stay with luminous yellow. The other colours lack impact.

Fountain pens
Years ago on internal flights in Russia passengers were given cellophane tubes in which to place their fountain pens in case they leaked with the change in pressurisation. Although fountain pens function better than ball pens they still, in the vast majority of cases, leak. Not recommended for air travel as the ink will invariably get on your fingers, if not all over your pocket or briefcase.

Briefcases
The ideal briefcase has yet to be built. I have tried various styles and formats and I am currently engaged in a lively correspondence with a briefcase designer who swears he has cracked it. What do I find wrong with briefcases?

If they are strong enough they are too heavy.

I have a splendid American case made out of industrial belting leather which can stand up to all the hard wear that can be handed out. However, empty it is almost too heavy to carry around. Loaded up it becomes a burden.

If they are light enough they break.

My experience has been that many of the mass produced briefcases available abroad suffer from inferior fittings which snap under load.

They look inelegant.

Not the Gucci case, which approaches the ultimate in style in briefcases. It is one of the few briefcases that I have ever seriously wanted. (The other is made by Bally in Switzerland.) The founder of Gucci once said that the quality is remembered long after the price is forgotten. He is probably right.

They let everything slide to the bottom.

I've got around this by building a sub-framework inside my case so that my dictating machine, calculator, pens, papers, cameras and refills don't all end up in a messy heap at the bottom of the briefcase. My adaptation (made from plastic curtain rods) is not patented.

Always consider the possibility that you do not need a briefcase at all. In his book *Power* Michael Korda wrote that the power of the executive was in inverse proportion to the thickness of his briefcase. This may well be true. Harold S. Geneen of ITT, according to popular myth, never carried a briefcase at all and he ran one of the largest companies in the world. I once saw Nubar Gulbenkian Jr—at that time one of the richest men in the world through being heir to a large oil fortune—striding from his Rolls Royce to an important meeting with his papers contained in a tatty brown manila folder.

Microscopes
There are several relatively low power microscopes—30X magnifying power—on the market (one manufacturer is Sasco, another is sold by Tandy) and they have a wondrous effect when used to examine supplier's goods. It gives a spurious impression of expertise on the part of the buyer.

Dictating machines
Despite protestations by manufacturers to the contrary, it is almost impossible to dictate on a dictating machine when flying. The noise of the engines intrudes. Elsewhere, a dictation machine acts as an excellent notebook and helps the busy executive keep in touch with his home office. The amount of paperwork that can be ploughed through in one hour is quite amazing once you have got the hang of dictating. It is a minor art and one well worth acquiring.

I use the Philips C195 for dictation and the office uses the Philips 0186 for transcription. There are several Japanese versions that perform the same function but note well that the cassettes are *not* interchangeable. Philips does not work on Pearl and vice versa.

Portable music systems
The music system on most aircraft is far from ideal. If you are in Economy Class you will be asked by some airlines on certain sectors to rent a set of plastic tube earphones which are known, not with affection, as 'brain squeezers'. The second problem is that the choice of music frequently leaves much to be desired and often has nothing to do with that listed in the inflight programme.

One answer to this problem lies with the ubiquitous Sony Walkman (and all the clones that it has inspired). Wearing this splendid portable music instrument, you can listen to your own brand of music—Welsh choirs, brass bands, Gilbert and Sullivan,

Deep Purple, Elvis Costello—in high fidelity. I have seen in America, but not yet in Australia, a device which allows you to link your electronic earphones to the aircraft's sound system and thus avoid the 'brain squeezers'. It does not appear to be available in Australia yet.

Cameras
Every business executive should carry a small camera. It is useful as a visual notebook—pictures of displays, damaged goods, shopping arcades—and it is equally useful as a way of saying a polite thank you to your hosts. 'Here are some pictures I took at the delightful dinner . . .' The simpler and smaller the camera the better, provided it uses 35mm film. I use the 35mm Minox on business trips, but there are several types available, of which the Olympus is recommended by those who have used it. Both of these machines can be supplied with a small battery powered flash. Almost indispensable.

3

Dealing with the dangers

Danger for danger's sake is senseless.

Leigh Hunt

It's wrong to paint too dark a picture. Incorrect to stress the nasty possibilities. Unfair to list nothing but the dangers. But it nevertheless remains true that tourists are more likely to get robbed and ripped off than most people.

It has never happened to you. It probably never will happen to you. But there are certain precautions you can take to weigh the odds even further in your favour. And before I start sounding like someone who knows it all and always gets it right, let me tell you a sad and salutary tale.

A friend of mine, Tony Martarano, who is a photographer, an American and quite large, was going to work for a while in the Philippines. Part of the time he would be at Clark Field, the US Air Force base which abuts Angeles City, a well-known hangout for desperates and crims. I advised him that his best bet when going out at night into the sinful darkness was to keep a small amount of money, say 300 pesos, in his top shirt pocket, and keep the rest of his valuables in a nylon pouch strapped firmly to his ankle.

On his very first night on the town a jeepney driver swerved his vehicle into a side street and Martarano was surrounded by three thugs with knives. Their first words were, 'OK, fat boy, off

with the boots and socks.' The advice that follows, therefore, is not guaranteed to be infallible. Just helpful.

Before you leave on a trip, make two photocopies of your airline tickets, the relevant pages of your passport, any relevant insurance forms, your travellers' cheques and your credit cards. One set goes to someone you trust. The other set goes into a large brown envelope which is taped to the inside of your suitcase. Then, if you do get turned over, you can replace essential items with some ease.

Leave your flash jewellery at home. Brainwash yourself into believing that wearing anything but junk jewellery on holiday is vulgar ostentation.

Use the hotel's safe for valuables. It may be a pain in the bum checking things in and out, but it is better than losing them.

Never let anyone have your passport for any reason. Hang on to it like grim death. Your passport is worth quids to naughty persons of evil intent.

Do not use designer suitcases. Although I much admire Louis Vuitton, using a genuine product of that company while travelling is asking for trouble. In the trade they are called 'steal-me cases', as are Haliburton and other 'flash'.

Do not use an American Express gold card. Every time I write this I get an anguished letter from the marketing department of American Express saying that, firstly, the theft of gold cards is no greater than that of the ordinary kind and, secondly, I do not realise the extra advantages of the gold over the green.

To the first, I answer that police in many countries in Asia say that a gold card is one way that thieves spot potential victims. Some of my shadier friends confirm this. And to the second, I reply that this is, indeed, true. I have always thought a gold card a vulgar ostentation only attractive to the *nouveau riche*. But in this, as in much else, I may well be wrong.

If, when out walking, a voice from a car—friendly or otherwise—tries to attract your attention, get well back from the vehicle before replying. You need to be far enough away so that you cannot be dragged into the car.

The nice friendly couple you meet in the park who are so concerned over your health and welfare may, indeed, be exactly what you think. On the other hand, someone may be setting you up for the Iron Mattress. This unpleasant confidence trick sees you being taken home to an apparently respectable middle-class apartment. Then, depending how it is played, you may be offered a massage, a lie-down, a view of the antiques in the other room—during which time your belongings will be rifled.

The strange name of this ploy comes from the fact that, in its original version, it was carried out by a young lady who appeared to fall helplessly in love with the big/brave/strong/handsome tourist. While this situation was discussed on the mattress the lady's true inamorata was rifling the hapless punter's trouser pockets.

Do not think that this cannot happen to you. It has happened to two perfectly respectable photographers—one male, one female—of my acquaintance in Sydney. And to dozens of other people I know around the world.

Check every bill. Recently I had two blatant attempts to rip me off—both, as it happens, in San Francisco. This is now a universal problem. The working hypothesis seems to be: here is a tourist ripe for plucking, let us pluck.

Make sure that anything you buy is wrapped before your very eyes. There is a sadly prevalent habit of wrapping other, cheaper goods up while your back is turned. If you are rushing to the airport, a brick, instead of a video camera, is not unknown.

Do not fight if you are robbed. The thieves are stronger, faster and more desperate than you are. Two young English police inspectors on holiday in Manila. A thief picks the pocket of one who turns and grabs the malefactor ... and ends up with a knife in his gut. Do not fight for your wallet. Wallets are easily replaced. Your life is not.

Do not ever, ever, under any circumstances, carry anything overseas for anyone you do not know—or for anyone you know for that matter. Not unless you know precisely what you are carrying and have seen it in the raw and unpacked state. And probably not even then. Smuggling for other people carries exactly the same penalties as smuggling for yourself.

Most crimes occur where lights are of a reddish hue and where you, the mug punter, are somewhat incapacitated by the effects of the demon grog. The policy of virtue and perfection would be to never go to such places of low repute. If, however, like me, you are easily led astray, only carry enough cash for your evening's cavortings. Leave the rest in the safe back at the hotel.

Pay as you go. Always, in a bar, pay for every round of drinks as they are served. Then there are no nasty arguments when a bill is provided at the end of the evening with the Mama-san's birthday counted in.

If any of your baggage is extra valuable keep a close eye on it, even when you think it is in safe hands. Les Bell tours the world giving seminars. He carries with him a most desirable and covetable Toshiba T3100 computer. At a London hotel recently, the friendly hall porter took the computer at the front door and left by the back, never to be seen again.

If someone tells you that disaster has struck, take special care. A singularly nasty trick at London airports is to spot a mug punter queuing at the currency exchange and run an ice-cream cone down the back of this person's jacket. As he twists out of the jacket to check the damage, the miscreant runs away with the briefcase.

Always carefully destroy or file the carbon copy of your credit card charge. Then no one can use the number to order goods and services.

Do not leave your baggage unattended at airports. Not for a moment. Take it into the loo with you.

4

Money and insurance

For the love of money is the root of all evil; which while some coveted after, they have erred from the faith, and pierced themselves through with many sorrows.

Timothy, 1.

If you are travelling you can get much greater value for your money by choosing with care how you will carry your money with you and how you will pay your bills.

How to take your money with you. There are six methods of which I am aware. There may be more.

Advance payment

Pay for as much as possible in advance. I am all for tour packages which save money—and most of them do. For example, in going to Tahiti you would be out of your tree to use anything but a package tour. Try to get everything possible included and pay for it before you leave. This way you will get the advantage of the operator's superior purchasing power and you will know, going in, roughly what the total cost will be.There are those who sneer at package travel. Not me. I use it all the time and it saves me serious money.

Credit cards

If you are going abroad you need one good credit card. Before you leave make sure that bills will be settled monthly or that you

have a very large credit limit. There is a reason for this. When you check into a hotel your credit card is swiped. The hotel then makes a credit claim for what it thinks you will spend during your stay. Hotels rarely amend this to the amount that you spend. This does not mean that you pay extra to the hotel but your credit swiftly disappears. You need a large credit limit on a card to avoid this problem if you are staying at several different hotels. American Express, which has no credit limit, does not have this problem.

The most widely accepted credit card in my experience is Visa. Even this card can have minor problems. Recently in a hypermarket in France an Englishman, Philip Scott, wheeled a trolley piled with goods to the check-out point. The till had a big sign saying Visa cards were accepted. The checker rejected the Visa card because it did not have enough numbers. In conversation with Philip I found out that Barclay's Bank had issued this card in England. On comparing cards I found his had 13 digits. Mine has 16 digits. As I understand it, many electronic checking systems will not take a 13-digit card.

You can also use Visa for drawing cash from your account in most countries of the world.

The next most widely accepted card is American Express which also has a cheque-cashing facility which works somewhat differently from that of Visa.

Note carefully that many restaurants in the United States and

Europe will not accept a credit card of any description. They say this is because of the percentage that goes to the card company. I am quite certain it is because the restaurants concerned are all on a cash tax fiddle. Credit cards are not as universally used in West Germany and Austria as they are in other countries. Check all your credit card bills most carefully. Smaller establishments have been known to alter the figures after you have signed.

Travellers' cheques

These are safe and can be easily replaced if you mislay them. Provided you have the list of numbers kept safely somewhere else. I always photocopy the list and keep it in my suitcase separately. The original list I keep in my passport. Then, if anything should happen, I can rattle off the numbers and easily get a replacement. For example American Express, which claims 44 per cent of the market share, has more than 90 000 refund points.

I am not enamoured of travellers' cheques in Australian dollars. I sometimes find that the only easy place to exchange them is the hotel cashier's desk and the rates there are always, but always, ruinous. If I am using this method I get destination cheques—ones issued in the currency of the country which I am visiting. That way I know the exchange rate before I start.

In some countries you pay a penalty rate on travellers' cheques—most of Scandinavia, France and parts of West Germany—while in others you get a small improvement in the rates. Most shops will accept travellers' cheques in payment of goods. The rates you get will not be favourable. If you are a worry-wart and scared of losing cash then travellers' cheques will probably do you very nicely.

Only get American Express, Thomas Cook, First National or cheques plainly endorsed with a Visa stamp. All others can be difficult to change—impossible in some countries. Note that in England, the banks are very peculiar about issuing travellers' cheques. The National Westminster—a blight take them—baulked at issuing me with a serious amount of money in travellers' cheques. A snotty bank teller told me I should use the bank's letter of credit system instead. As I was travelling to Burma this was of little help.

In certain countries there is a surcharge added for changing travellers' cheques. The situation is a fluid one, but European countries are the worst offenders.

Sweden charges as high as six per cent and France follows not too far behind. In taking travellers' cheques to these countries you are effectively losing a substantial percentage of your money before you start.

Certain travellers' cheques are difficult to cash if the issuing house is not widely known. For example, Westpac travellers' cheques are widely accepted in the People's Republic of China, but not necessarily in every other country. Your bank manager should be able to advise you what travellers' cheques are acceptable where but if in doubt ask your travel agent.

Letter of credit

Have your bank manager write you a letter of credit which can be cashed at a corresponding bank in another country. These instruments of financial conveyance are now fairly archaic, although they are still used by members of the older generation who remember making The Trip with Letters of Credit firmly filed away with Letters of Introduction to the Right People.

Bank transfer

In theory you can have money transferred to you in any country by electronic transfer. In practice this can take five full working days. Even using telephonic transfer it can take five working days, despite the assurances of bank employees who have plainly never been at the sharp end. In some countries—the Philippines is a good example—it is almost impossible to get a bank transfer without an unacceptable amount of *sturm und drang*. Avoid this if you can.

Cash

For years I have carried cash with me around the world and I have never had my pocket picked or lost my wallet. I carry the wallet in an inside pocket which is closed with a big safety pin. Deep in my wallet I have a $US100 bill which is there in case of dire emergencies. Otherwise I use Australian dollars and change them as I need them. This may not give the most advantageous rate of exchange but it is by far the most convenient method of carrying money.

On your return to Australia change any foreign currency you have left at the airport. The rate charged by banks to change foreign money can only be described as usury.

It is most important that you quickly get into a mind set where you realise that any money—no matter what the currency—has real value. There is a desperate temptation when abroad to think of the local currency as 'funny money'. It is nothing of the sort. You worked just the same number of hours to earn it as you did for its Australian equivalent.

Travel insurance

You can insure against almost any mishap that can happen on your travels—including loss of cash up to $500. Other insurances in order of importance are:

Medical cover: obvious because if you become ill in, say , the United States the costs can bankrupt you. Additional expenses caused by illness: again, these mount up if one member of the party has to stay on in a hotel while the other has an appendix removed. A good insurance policy should also cover medical costs after you return to Australia.

Loss of deposits through cancellation, including cancellation due to jury service.

Baggage: this can be insured up to and above $3000. It is important to note that the airline's cover for baggage lost or destroyed is not high. Loss of money and travel documents, cover up to $500 will probably meet the situation.

Personal accident and personal liability insurances are a must, especially in some countries (notably in the Middle East) where no matter what happens in an accident the visitor is always at fault.

Strike action which directly or indirectly affects your travel plans can be insured against.

Look for worldwide representation when buying your insurance. This is essential if you want your claims dealt with speedily and efficiently.

How much should this cost you? For an insurance policy which covers all these contingencies and a few others for a four week period the price should be something under $100. A small price to pay for peace of mind.

Duty-free shopping

That I am a liar, a convincing liar, is well known. The talent in this area comes through being born in Wales. Part of one's heritage. Most of my lies are what I like to think of as beneficial lies. I have, for example, always taught my children that the ice-cream van only plays its bell when sold out. Another excellent lie is that, because I travel overseas more than nine times a year, I am classified by Australian Customs as a professional traveller. Therefore, I automatically lose all my duty-free allowances. I have told this lie so convincingly over the years that my relatives and friends believe me totally. They never ask me to do duty-free shopping for them when I am overseas.

This is a beneficial lie because most duty-free shopping is, in truth, a snare and a delusion. Duty free rarely lives up to the promise of the name. It is normally a very expensive way to save money. Duty-free shops are seen by airport authorities around the world as milch cows which are there for milking. The general way of improving the poor cow's yield is as follows. The airport is under the control of an airport authority—normally a branch of the government. This authority, like all authorities, has trouble making ends meet, trouble keeping within a budget. Therefore, it lets out store space in the airport to the highest bidder. There is normally no discussion about fitness to serve, honesty, probity, track record of service to the customer. That does not come into it. Instead the only criterion used to judge a duty-free store is how much it is willing to pay. The highest bidder gets the contract, no debate.

The bidding for these rights has become frantic and frenetic simply because of the magic effect that the words duty free have on travellers. I have seen hundreds of shoppers at Hong Kong and other airports buying goods that they would never dream of acquiring under other circumstances. And paying top dollar for the privilege.

The worst offenders in this respect are the Japanese. For most of them it is their first and very probably their last trip overseas. On the face of it the prices in the duty-free stores are very low — compared with the Ginza. So the Japanese buy, buy, buy. An added complication is that the average Japanese holiday traveller is designer-label mad and this adds to the duty-free bonanza.

The prices of the contracts to set up a duty-free shop reflect the profits that can be made selling to these mug punters.

The current world record for shop rights is that paid by Duty Free Shoppers—a company that specialises in this area—for the concession at Honolulu. This came to a mind-numbing $US1 billion. An executive of the same company told me that it had built the airport in Saipan for nothing, in exchange for the exclusive right to run the duty-free store at that airport, which has a very significant Japanese trade. Plainly these huge sums are but part of an equation. The other part means that the price of everything sold in these stores has a very substantial loading. So substantial can be that percentage that duty free may be the phrase but not the reality. In some airports the prices of the goods in the duty-free stores are measurably higher than in the supermarkets in the same city.

Note also that the phrase 'duty free' means many things to many people. I am open to correction on this but almost the only genuine duty-free shops, which are not in an airport or a port, are in Australia. These were certainly the first true 'duty-free' stores off-site. You will see many 'duty-free' stores in New York City. Within the meaning of the Act they are nothing of the sort. The same is true of Lautoka in Fiji. These stores are 'duty free' only in name.

How, then, do you avoid being ripped off in a duty-free store?

Some basics:

Make sure you are in a genuine duty-free store. In almost every other country in the world this means they will be in an airport or on a ship. In Sydney some genuine duty-free stores exist in the city.

Ignore the siren call of duty free. As a matter of sober fact I fly around the world several times a year and I rarely, if ever, buy anything duty free. I do not believe it is worth the hassle of buying and the strain of carrying. Saving a few dollars on a bottle of Scotch does nothing for me if I have to lug it halfway round the world.

Bear in mind that you can go broke saving money. Ask yourself very carefully whether you truly need the bumper economy gallon size of Eau de Frisson. Or whether you have taken leave of your senses because you are travelling on holiday.

Know your prices

There is no way in the world that you can make a proper evaluation of a 'bargain' unless you know the price you would pay under normal circumstances. It is important that you compare apples with apples. Helen Hutcheon, my favourite travel person, was with me in Fiji and she had with her a list of all the prices of all the goods she might be tempted to buy. Out of interest, the duty-free stores in Fiji came out of this comparison so unfavourably that she did not buy a thing. The important point is that she went in prepared.

For anything where a guarantee is important—shop in Australia. In theory, there are international guarantees. In practice getting them fulfilled is sometimes a great hassle. If you insist on buying a 35mm SLR camera, buy it in Australia before you leave at a duty-free store. You will have an Australian guarantee. This beats an international guarantee as a royal flush beats two pairs.

- Never buy any 'designer' goods which would appeal to the Japanese market The Japanese are designer-label mad and the prices in duty-free shops always reflect this.
- Watch the exchange rate. If you allow the duty-free store to change currency for you, take it as read that it will not be at the most favourable bank rate. Favourable to you, that is.
- Know where you will get the best prices. My unofficial league table for duty-free prices, based on careful scrutiny is:
  1. Brisbane.
  2. Downtown Sydney.
  3. Perth.
  4. Dubai - known by Qantas in-flight crews as Marlboro country.
  5. Schipol airport, Amsterdam—low prices and wide range. There are a lot of airports fighting to be at the bottom of my list. It would be a damn close run thing between Tokyo, Fiji, Hong Kong and London Heathrow. My guess is that Heathrow gets the guernsey—but only after a recount.

5

On the cheap

And make me travel forth without my cloak,
To let base clouds o'ertake me in my way.
William Shakespeare, *The Sonnets*

Let me worry you with some true life stories.

I sat in the Champs Elysées at an outdoor café. The sun was warm on my face. The famous smell of chestnuts was not in the air. Instead, it was carbon monoxide. A waiter hovered. I ordered, in my best French, a beer. It was a cold, light lager. It cost $17.80.

In Hong Kong on the Kowloon side, two young Australians walk into a girlie bar in the late afternoon. They order a beer each. Two hostesses say hello and without further ado order themselves two glasses of green tea. When the two Australians want to leave the bill is $85 and violent action is threatened unless it is paid.

In Athens a taxi driver drives me 213 metres (I paced out the distance the next day) and demands 1000 drachmas for the journey. Something around $9.

An Australian couple takes a taxi from downtown Tokyo to Narita airport during the rush hour. The taxi fare is $480. They query this and find the normal rate is between $200 and $250.

In London airport my belt snaps and I race into the duty-free store to buy a replacement. When I get to the check-out counter the unsmiling assistant asks for $143. At that price my trousers

can fall down around my ankles for all I care.

These horror stories happened because of lack of prior information about costs. They all teach one lesson most clearly. You must check the price of any services or goods before you buy.

Desperate economy stakes

The cost of travelling breaks down into three areas: those totally outside your control; those you can partly control; those where you make decisions.

Costs totally outside your control applies, for example, to flying around Australia. Although there are different categories of fares they are fixed fares. True we now have deregulation but the expected massive drops in air fares have simply not yet happened. Possibly matters will improve as we go along. Until we have true open slather and a proper free market your costs are fixed and there is little you can do about it. The same applies to Eurailpass and prepackaged holidays.

Costs you can partly control include those incurred in hotels. The published rate for a room, called the rack rate in the trade, is the opening stage in the bargaining process. Unless the hotel is booked solid then rack rates can normally be negotiated. They are discounted as a matter of course for corporate accounts, tour packagers and for members of certain travel clubs. For example, membership of the Qantas club Connections can get you discounts at various hotels around the world.

The same applies to hire car rates. There is a fixed basic rate and then a raft of special offers floating somewhere below. Getting those discounts may only require that you be a member of a frequent flyer club. Most times I boldly state it as a fact and I am rarely asked to show documentation to back it up.

Costs you can completely control include these examples.

When Roy Thomson went to Britain to set up his newspaper and television empire he stayed at The Savoy. Every morning he got up, dressed and went and had breakfast at a cab drivers' diner. That was a cost he could control.

Sir Stanley Unwin, the man who ran the publishing company Allen and Unwin with style and great economy, told me that he had never taken a taxi in his life. We were lunching in Joe Lyons at the time. Joe Lyons is not an up-market restaurant. Again, costs that could be controlled.

My offsider, Matt Whelan, and I were in Singapore. It was his first visit. I offered to pay for the food if he paid for the drinks. For dinner I took him to the Satay Club where we ate with both trotters in the trough for $11. We then had drinks in the lounge of the Hyatt—that set Matt back $38.

In every hotel in the world I bring in my own grog, wash my own clothes, sort out my own, non-hotel breakfast. I control the costs.

Travelling on the smallest of budgets is not difficult. All it requires is a Scottish attitude towards the spending of money and a flexible attitude towards creature comforts. I have been the most impoverished of world travellers. I was, at that time, working for airlines writing and producing audio visual shows. My net worth was something less than nil. I had to get around most of the countries of the world on the smell of an oily rag in order to fulfil the contract and dig myself out of my financial hole. I managed and I managed, though I say so myself, most successfully.

Desperate economy stakes—food

My own system is as follows. First, I carry with me a supply of Campbell's Cup-a-Soup, a packet of muesli, a packet of dried milk powder, some tea bags, UHT milk portions in plastic sachets, a small electric water immersion heater and an enamel mug. With that little lot I can, and have, travelled the world without once paying for a meal. The heater will work from any socket as I have it fixed with a universal plug (obtainable at almost all airport shops). Most supermarkets sell Dairy Farmer UHT Long Life milk portions.

I soak the muesli overnight in a powdered milk-warm water mixture and have it for breakfast. This is followed by a quiet and contemplative cup of tea with the UHT milk as extra flavouring. Powdered milk does not work as well. I have a cup of soup for lunch, spring vegetable being my current favourite although I am willing to listen to a good argument for chicken and noodles. Finally I have another cup of soup for dinner.

Dieticians will throw up their hands in horror but I also take multivitamin tablets and eat a lot of fruit that I buy from street stalls. This is not the sort of diet I would recommend to anyone over a long period of time but for short trips of three weeks or so it is perfectly feasible.

Now that I have recovered from my somewhat straitened financial circumstances I still carry all the same gear with me. I write this on a flight to Harare in Zimbabwe. Ironically, I am in first class on Qantas and they are feeding me in the stuffed Strasbourg goose mode. But I have with me all the makings and if I find myself in a hotel with outrageous food prices I will switch back to my minimalist diet with no qualms whatsoever.

If I am eating out I find that grazing—eating food from street stalls—gets me a wide range of excellent tucker at a very low price. In some cities such as Bangkok and New York grazing can give you a low cost gourmet feast—although heartburn may follow. Grazing is possible in almost any city with the two exceptions of Edinburgh and Geneva.

In most European cities a drink consumed at the bar will be a third of the cost of one imbibed at a table. Practise drinking standing up.

Desperate economy stakes—drink

Although I appreciate the cooling amber fluid and have been known to wax rhapsodic over a Cabernet Merlot I can quite happily leave it totally alone. This is the ideal solution.

Never use the minibar installed enticingly in your hotel room. The temptation of a drink from this construct of the devil should be sternly resisted. First, it is an antisocial habit and brings drinking into bad repute. Second, the price is ridiculous.

Depending on the country and the hotel, the cost of a Scotch can be as much as $5 and $2 for a soft drink seems to be standard. Even when I am travelling at someone else's expense, I never use the minibar in the room. Instead, I drink in a local bar, not that of the hotel, as all good Australians should.

I also carry with me a half bottle of whisky and drink it with ice from the hotel bedroom fridge—for which there is no charge—and water, also free. Some distilleries are now offering half bottles of straight malt in plastic containers which seems to me to be ideal. I buy the drink from a duty-free shop.

Desperate economy stakes—ground travel

Do not use the hotel's transport. Especially to and from the airport. Not unless it is a bus and you know the price or it is part of a package and included in the total price. Typically, the charge will be two or three times that of a taxi.

There are very few cities in the world where any form of locomotion can beat walking. (Los Angeles is one example that springs to mind, Manila another). In many cities walking is faster than any other means of getting around. This is true in New York, most Italian and many other European cities. Plan all your activities so that you can walk to where you want to go. It is healthy, you meet a better class of person, you save a lot of money. Your only investment will be a small map which you should buy as soon as you arrive. Note that many travel and tourist organisations give these maps away for nothing.

If you cannot walk to your destination, because of distance or weather, use public transport. In some cities public transport is vastly superior to any other mode of transportation. For example, in Hong Kong if you use a taxicab instead of the Mass Transit Railway to get around you are barmy.

Desperate economy measures—laundry

To my knowledge I have never sent any item of clothing to a hotel laundry. This has been challenged but as far as I know it is a correct statement. Laundries in hotels create problems.

First they are ruinously expensive. Hotels do not want to offer the service. They try to discourage you by charging more for laundering a garment than you paid for buying it.

Second they destroy garments. All European hotels use ultra hot irons for taking the wrinkles out of shirts. This melts the lining in shirt collars and results in unsightly bubbles. As well, the pressing machine puts such a weight on the buttons that they crack and break.

Third, hotel laundries never deliver the goods back when you need them—always an hour later.

In most of Asia and much of the US, it is cheaper to buy a new shirt than to have one washed and ironed. Anyone who does not wash their smalls in the hotel wash-basin is not, in my book, a true traveller. Most hotels supply soap powder. Every evening, when I get back to my hotel, I fill the bath with warmish water, throw in my day's clothes with some soap powder and practise running on the spot.

This serves two purposes. It gets my clothes squeaky clean and it gives me some much needed exercise. All my shirts are drip dry so they do not need ironing. I hang mine to dry overnight over the bath and, if necessary, finish them off with the hair dryer.

For larger items, find a local laundromat. This is a technique used by David Dale, the ex-editor of *The Bulletin*. He keeps all his dirty clothes for one week and then finds a laundromat. This saves money and, sometimes, affords him an excellent story. His account of his adventures in trying to find a laundromat in Salt Lake City is a joy to read.

Dry-cleaning and pressing

I am opposed to paying money to have my clothes pressed. When I unpack my case, if there are any wrinkles I hang the clothes in the bathroom with the hot water running and close the door firmly. The result is better than any pressing. The steam takes out all the wrinkles. This advice does not endear me to hotel managements, but it works.

I keep the amount of clothes I carry to a minimum.

On this trip I have three pairs of light fawn trousers from Marks and Spencers in England. These are washable and have a slight stretch. Unlike traditional Australian moleskins they fit as if tailored. I can wash them myself if they get dirty. I restore the crease by folding them and leaving them under the mattress overnight. This is a trick taught me by a sergeant in the Coldstream Guards. It is not easy to achieve and needs practice. If you ever meet an ex-guardsman ask for a demonstration.

To go with these trousers is one grey jacket cut like a blazer in a wool/cashmere mixture. This never shows wrinkles.

With this little lot I will be able to explore the Victoria Falls tomorrow, go on to Kariba and then return to Harare on Tuesday to hold a seminar. And I will, I promise you, look quite the natty gent.

Desperate economy measures—telephones

Do not make interstate or international telephone calls from a hotel telephone. Not until you have ascertained the charges.

This came smartly to my attention when I stayed recently at the North British Hotel in Edinburgh. A call to Australia was charged to me at three times the cost of the call. Such a monstrous impost is common throughout Europe. In almost every major European hotel, telephone calls are doubled or tripled before being added to your bill. The European equivalent of Telecom, no doubt, wants you to reach out and touch someone. But their hotels want to reach out and touch you. The surcharges used in Australia are much more reasonable, but can still add a hefty extra charge to your final bill if you are not careful.

In Sydney, for example, the Inter-Continental Hotel charges 70 cents for a local call, $3 minimum for operator assistance on a reverse charge, and adds 35 per cent to interstate and international calls. The Sheraton-Wentworth charges 70 cents a local call with a surcharge on interstate and international calls. The Holiday Inn Menzies charges 50 cents a local call and has a mark-up, unspecified, on interstate and international calls. The Regent charges 70 cents for local calls, 90 cents a minute for interstate calls, and $3 a minute for most overseas calls. One hotel in

Sydney charges 100 per cent on all international calls up to the first $40.

Almost every hotel in Australia has coin and, often, credit-card telephones downstairs in reception. Many now have OTC telephones that work with credit cards in the same area. All emphasise these are available for guests. Some go out of their way to advise guests that it is cheaper to use these inconvenient public telephones than to call from their own room.

In Asia, the prices are much the same as in Australia. In the US, they tend to be even more reasonable. This is because many hotels have entered into an agreement with AT&T, the American telecommunications giant, to keep prices to a low and uniform level. But in Europe, it is sucker season for telephoning guests. When you check into almost any European middle-level hotel, you will see a queue waiting somewhat impatiently at the lobby telephones. They consist of guests engaged in saving large amounts of money.

Never, ever use a hotel telephone. And it is no good trying to get around this by using credit cards or reverse charges. The hotel whack on a big handling fee for each of these. Note that in some countries, in some hotels, you are charged whether you make a connection or not.

Desperate economy measures—accommodation

The most expensive hotels are always near the airport. The cheapest are always near the central railway station. All chain hotels are expensive except in America where some of the motel groups are bargain priced.

At almost every airport in the world and at most railway stations there is a Travellers' Aid desk or equivalent. The people staffing the booth will help you get a room for the night at the right price.

No matter which hotel you stay at, check your bill carefully. It is not that the hotel will pad out your bill to make a greater profit—this practice is almost unknown. It is rather that miscellaneous charges will be added to your account by an idle/confused/incompetent assistant cashier. If you check carefully on the morning of your departure, you will often earn the hotel staff's frowns and barely concealed disapproval. They believe their role in life is to get guests away as quickly as possible. This is admirable, but leads to a less admirable impatience with guests who prudently check their bill.

How often is it wrong?

Judging from my extensive experience and those of fellow travellers—I belong to a group that gives seminars and we all travel to Europe and Asia at least four times a year—a serious error will occur 10 to 20 per cent of the time.

Even though I have sworn a blood oath never to use a mini-bar, the charges appear with monotonous regularity. Even though I only telephone from a call box or a post office, except in an emergency, I find phantom calls listed on bills with gay abandon. When you query such an entry, your challenge may be met with an air of impolite disbelief. Persist and your bill will be adjusted. Such persistence pays dividends.

Desperate economy measures—money

If you do not have money in your pocket you do not spend it. Only change as much money as you need. Do not make allowances for splurges.

Never change money at the hotel. The rates are ruinous. Instead change at a bank at the railway station or the airport. Note the rates carefully. Many money changers—they were the ones that Christ quite correctly whipped out of the temple—add a handling charge for each transaction and show this in very small print indeed.

Always count your change. Short-changing travellers is a way of life in some countries.

Always know exactly what the currency is worth in Australian dollars. There is a tendency to treat foreign bank notes as funny money. It is not. It is Australian dollars in a different guise.

Desperate economy measures—toiletry goods

What follows I am ashamed to admit. I function almost totally on free toiletry kits issued by the airlines. The very best are those supplied by Qantas in first class which is in a real leather case and by British Airways at the pointy end. I have a fond spot for the free toilet kit of Air Mauritius. Most hotels these days supply free shampoo which I collect like a bower bird.

Economy measures - do they work in practice?

It depends on the country. Let us look first at England and then at Paris.

In New York, I was told the key to success was to think Yiddish, dress English and look Irish. The key to a cheap and successful holiday in Britain is to stay at bed and breakfasts, lunch at pubs and dine Indian. Which cries out for further explanation.

Bed and breakfasts first.

This is a peculiarly British institution (although I have seen some pale Australian imitations) where private houses take in guests as a small commercial sideline, which I am quite sure is never brought to the attention of the tax inspector.

Bed and breakfasts vary (as, indeed, the people of Britain vary). But you will always find them in tourist areas. Houses with discreet cardboard signs in the front window, decorously tucked in front of the lace curtain and offering bed and breakfast.

The bed is normally double and shares the room with a large wardrobe. The facilities, as they are euphemistically called, are shared. The breakfast is a cholesterol-loaded feast that will see you through the day with no pangs of hunger. The cost is minimal. All of which are benefits, but there is more.

The people who offer bed and breakfasts are the people of Britain. Not snotty hoteliers with their hands ever ready for a tip and a vestigial command of the English language. My Mam offered bed and breakfasts. So did all our neighbours.

Staying in these homes introduces you to the warp and weft of life in England as no other experience can. It was at a bed and breakfast that I first tried to play the bagpipes. It was at a bed and breakfast that I learned the fascination of campanology—bell ringing to the rest of you—and the mathematical intricacies of a Treble Bob Major. Regardless of what business I am doing in Britain or who is paying, wherever possible, I opt for a bed-and-breakfast establishment.

If you travel to broaden the mind, to meet the people, to embrace new experiences, bed and breakfasts are the way to go.

Pubs for lunch? Where else?

Pubs in Britain have changed dramatically in the past few months with the advent of civilised licensing hours, and less dramatically over the past few years with the changing of tastes and living styles among the great British beer-drinking public. But the basics are still there.

British pubs are clubs. Locals drink at—the precise phrase—their 'local', which is normally within walking distance. This has great advantages in a day when the random breath test looms large on the horizon. The people each side of the bar know each other, are tolerant of eccentricities and idiosyncrasies. There are no rules for membership of these clubs. All it takes is time and acceptance.

Opposite the British Museum in Russell Street is the Museum Tavern. Over the years, I have made a point of dropping in for the odd ale. I recognise several of the regulars. It is, in a sense, my local.

There is a buffet behind the bar which offers as wide a range of cold and hot foods as I have ever seen offered in a bar. I had two cold Scotch eggs—that most peculiar English dish—to go with my pint of bitter. This beer is unlike Australian beer. It is warm, has a strong taste, cannot be rushed. The British beer drinker is a contemplative cove. The beer moulds you that way.

This type of pub is repeated in its tens of thousands, throughout England.

You are feeling lonely in England? Front up to a bar, order a pint of best and a sandwich, then say, quietly but clearly: 'What do the British think about the Australians coming over here and buying up the newspapers and breweries?' You will be lonely no longer. This I promise you.

Dine Indian

Sounds strange advice, but is not.

Pubs are an English institution. Restaurants are not. The English eat out in a manner that is guilty, even furtive. (They approach sex in much the same manner, but that is a digression we shall avoid.)

They dine out as if their nanny had told them that enjoyment of food was not quite nice. As a result, good English restaurants—as opposed to good French restaurants in England—hardly exist. Those that do are written about in the serious Sunday newspapers as if they were a present miracle that should be experienced before they disappear. Which, indeed, they frequently do.

Good French or continental restaurants abound. The only problem is that you cannot afford to eat at them. My favourite (which I can afford only once on each visit) is L'Escargot in Greek Street. It has no exact equivalent in Australia, but then, there is no exact equivalent in Australia of the English dining out.

Bad so-called French and continental restaurants are a plague. The food they serve is unoriginal, something less than fresh, served with surly ill grace and it costs an arm and a leg.

There are exceptions. The only way you will find them is to use the *Egon Ronay Guide Book*, which is the only guide to eating out in Britain worth considering. Egon Ronay is a Hungarian and reading his books, you realise he is almost as much in despair for culinary Britain as I am.

All Chinese restaurants that I have ever tried in Britain have been quite dreadful and would not last a minute in Australia. My Cantonese friends from Hong Kong cannot believe how bad the Chinese food is in England.

But Indian food? Ah, that is something different. Even the smallest town in Britain will boast an Indian restaurant and the food served will be surprisingly good and cheap and does not always have to be belly-burning hot.

How much does this all cost?

My partner and I are travelling around England in a hired car. On average, we are spending about $50 a night for bed and breakfast for the two of us. Our pub lunches are coming to another $20. And our Indian meal in the evening comes to something around $30. For a little less than $100 a day, we sleep in elegant comfort, we eat most exceedingly well, we enjoy a plenitude of the cooling amber fluid and we meet the most interesting and eccentric people in the world.

For what more could a passionate traveller ask?

This is Paris

It is raining, which is as it should be. Paris rain is not as the rain of other cities. It is softer, benevolent. It caresses, rather than soaks.

When I first came to Paris to become involved in the running of an avant garde publishing house, Olympia Press, with Maurice Girodias, all Parisians took pride in not speaking English.

Certainly not to strangers. All this has now changed. In hotels, shops, restaurants—almost everyone speaks English. Indeed, they are quite pushy about it. And it is not just in the tourist-frequented areas. I am staying in an area called *Le Marais*—the marsh—which is some way out of the centre. The same availability of English still applies. This, I suppose, is one of the beneficial effects of the Common Market. An improvement.

Perhaps the main reason I come to Paris is because of the food. Not that I am a true gourmet. More a gourmand. It is perfectly possible to spend an arm and a leg on food in Paris. I am still in a state of shock after paying $17.80 for a single schooner of beer at Fouquet's. Granted, I was sitting on the pavement on the Champs Elysées and granted, I could have sat there all day. But the price is still ridiculous.

Normally I steer well away from such high-priced nonsenses and spend about what I would in Sydney.

My guide to eating out in Paris.

When you go to Paris—and you should go at least once in a lifetime—make your own discoveries. I am assured it is possible to get a bad meal in Paris. It is simply that it has never happened to me. At the following restaurants you will only get great meals.

First and foremost, La Crémerie Polidor. If it was good enough for Ernest Hemingway, James Joyce, André Gide, Paul Verlaine and Paul Valéry, it is good enough for me. For lunch yesterday I had the *plat du jour*, which was *cassoulet* in the classic style. This restaurant has never heard of nouvelle cuisine. Its style of cooking is still firmly embedded in the twenties. As are its decor and standard of service.

With my meal I had a *pichet*, a small jug, which is about a third of a bottle of Chateau Magondeau, a 1984 Grand Bordeaux, which has won a Medaille Concours Agricole and is well spoken of. A full bottle would have been silly, but a *pichet* at 30 francs, say $6.50, was just right. This system of serving excellent wines in less than bottle quantities is well worth cottoning on to. In most restaurants you can have a carafe of house wine, which normally will be singularly nasty and probably will have come from Algeria or Morocco and be chemically treated. You can drink it at a pinch. But you have to be desperate.

A step up from that is *réserve maison*, or *réserve du patron*. This is much better and very drinkable. At the top in quality and price are the wines which qualify for the title *vin délimité de qualité supérieur (VDQS)*, or *appellation d'origine controlée (AOC)*. These can be truly splendid wines, but can be pricey and a bottle too much to drink for one person.

Some restaurants serve great wines by the glass or small jug and the good ones get the Coupe de Meilleur Pot, which is a much-coveted award. This means that you can sample the grand wines of France—and grand wines, indeed, they are—without doing dire damage to either your wallet or your liver.

The best places to experience this superior plonk by the glass are in bars run by the Ecluse chain at 15 Quai des Grands-Augustins; 64 Rue Francois-1er and 15 Place de la Madeleine, both in the eighth arrondisement. They may have opened other branches by the time you get there. On offer are Bordeaux wines by the glass, some of them *grand cru*. These bars also have, beyond argument, the best chocolate.

Back to Polidor for the moment. The ideal time to front is around 1.30, when the first mad rush is over, but the atmosphere is still there. They don't accept telephone bookings.

To get to it, take the Métro to Odéon on Boulevard St Germain des Près and walk through Carrefour Odéon and then up Rue Monsieur le Prince to number 41. It is not a flashy frontage and easy to miss. The unisex toilets are very probably a historic monument.

After eating a literary lunch, go back down to St Germain des Près and turn left. You will shortly come to three great Paris institutions: Aux Deux Magots, the Café Flore and Brasserie Lipp. It was at Aux Deux Magots in 1964 and 1965 that I would often see Jean-Paul Sartre and Simone de Beauvoir hold literary court. She had long, frizzy, purple hair. Later, in England, to my great delight, I was able to publish the original paperback edition of de Beauvoir's *The Second Sex* which I have always considered to be the start of the sexual revolution.

And it was at the Café Flore that I met Juliette Greco and fell immediately and permanently in love.

You can have a glass of wine or a tea, typically with lemon, or a coffee and huddle over it for hours without disturbing the waiters of Aux Deux Magots, who have seen it all.

Always and ever you will see some tables occupied by Parisian lovers. They lean forward over the table with their spines concave, their buttocks jutting and their legs intertwined under the tables. Looks damned uncomfortable, but they do it by the hour. In Aux Deux Magots there was a dark-haired couple—both handsome—who were seemingly frozen eternally in this posture of adoration.

Let us, for the moment, move away from this passionate literary scene and look at a typical downmarket Paris restaurant.

Near my hotel is a restaurant called Le Chateaubriand on Avenue Parmentier. It specialises in the North African dish couscous. The clientele are basically the hard lads of the town. Several of them look as if they have frequently ridden all four horses of the Apocalypse. I sit down, order couscous and half a flagon of the house red. The owner, *le patron*, serves me himself. The food is excellent, but massively too much, the wine is Algerian rotgut and the bill 32 francs, a touch over $7.

If you are on a tight budget, there are many restaurants which serve better than acceptable food at these ludicrously low prices. One example is Chartier, in Montmartre, which is at 7 Rue du Faubourg Montmartre. Take the Métro to Montmartre, come out into Rue Montmartre and take the first turning on your left. This is an immense restaurant, which looks like a set designer's idea of a waiting room for the Orient Express—always crowded, always noisy. In the old French tradition, the waiter writes your order on the paper table-cloth. At dinner for two, one had fish soup (great), the other fresh shrimps (likewise), followed by veal (better than good) and shashlik (dreadful). To go with this, a bottle of Côtes de Provence rosé and some cheese to follow. Total price, 110 francs, under $25.

If you are on a very tight budget the answer is to picnic. Start off with a loaf of bread. These are called baguettes, cost three francs each, and were the glory of France. Sadly, they have in recent years deteriorated because the bakers do not like working through the night to make fresh batches. So they make them the day before and deep freeze them. Another black mark to progress. Baguettes, nevertheless, are still better than any bread that I have been able to find in Sydney.

To buy it, head for a *boulangerie*. Easy to find—they are everywhere and emit a glorious smell of warm bread. If you want the best baguettes, head for the shop with the biggest queues, Parisians know their bread.

Nearby will be a *charcuterie*—food shops in Paris come in clumps—where you can buy pâté, quiche, ham, saucissons (sausages) in all varieties, especially the dried, smaller kind. They will slice up the sausages for you. Many *charcuteries* also sell hot take-away dishes in plastic containers although I tend to avoid these as being too messy.

An example: for lunch in a *charcuterie* in the Rue du Faubourg du Temple I bought a portion of feuillette de jambon, six francs; a portion of museau de porc vinaigrette, four francs; some potato salad for three francs and a portion of salade Chinoise for five francs. There was enough there to feed me until I was full to groaning, for a total price of about $4.

Now, if you are a greater glutton than I, nip into the *fromagerie*, which will be somewhere on the same block, and experiment with cheeses you have never tried before. If you are quite open with the shopkeeper and confess ignorance you will sometimes find a selection of small portions being made up for you as a sampling kit.

Lastly, the wine. Standard French plonk as sold in supermarkets is not in the same race as the most basic of Australian flagon wines. The only one I have found which is consistently drinkable is Corbières. Better instead to treat yourself to a bottle with a cork in it. Again, tell the wine merchant the type of wine you want and that you are Australian and you are learning about French wines and you are poor. You will be pleasantly surprised at the friendly advice and assistance you will be given.

Where to eat your picnic? In the parks. There are dozens of them in Paris. In most you are not allowed to sit on the grass while you eat your lunch, but there are always park benches aplenty. On a recent trip I ate my picnic meals in the little park at the Pont Neuf end of the Ile de la Cité. Behind me, the Gothic wonders of Notre Dame. In front of me, the Seine.

I ate like a king in solitary splendour. I was alone, but I was not lonely, I had all of Paris around me.

6

Do you speak English? If not, why not?

You taught me language; and my profit on't
Is, I know how to curse; the red plague rid you,
For learning me your language!

William Shakespeare, *The Tempest*, I, ii,36

Bismarck was once told that a man could speak four languages fluently. 'What a very useful talent, ' he said. 'for a head waiter.' This sums up the attitude of most Australians to speaking foreign languages.

Speaking another language fluently is not easy. It is, indeed, extremely difficult. I am far from convinced that fluency, true fluency, in a foreign language is an unmixed blessing. For example, I have the severest doubts whether any mastery of the Japanese language by a non-Japanese will ever be regarded by the Japanese as more than non-relevant whimsy. Sometimes I feel that full fluency can be a decided drawback in business negotiations.

What does work and is worth acquiring, is sufficient grasp of any language to be able to deal with the basic essentials of travel. What is normally referred to as a smattering. Such a standard of fluency is not hard to acquire and not difficult to put into practice.

There is, of course, a problem. If you start speaking in a foreign language, even a few hesitant phrases, you will be

assumed to be fluent and will be met with a full, fine, frenzied flood of the language in return, spoken at breakneck speed. The first phrase to learn in any language is 'Please speak slowly. I do not understand your language.'

Being able to speak a language at this level is a politeness, an oiler of wheels, a smoother of the way. You will find that your hosts will appreciate that you have made the attempt and that the travelling life will become much easier, more pleasant. I have this smattering command in several languages and I am constantly trying to add more to my repertoire.

Accepting for the moment that some understanding of a language is a benefit on a holiday and on a business trip, how do you go about getting the required smattering? Several ways.

Fall in love .There is no better way of learning a language than having an intense affair with a partner who speaks no English.

Phrase books. The day when the phrase book taught you to say, 'The postillion has been struck by lightning' has passed. (Although a phrase book published in the Philippines and teaching Cebuano starts with a scene on a bus where you, the passenger, are asked if you will take a pig on your knee. And there is a language book for Indonesian where one of the scenarios is shopping for a single sock for a one-legged man. True.) The problem with phrase books is that they do not properly show the pronunciation and you can never find the right phrase when you need it.

Night school. With these it all depends on the quality of the teacher. I have known teachers who can make a language come alive, who can burn pronunciation and phrases into your memory bank, and I have known teachers who put you to sleep. What you need is a teacher like the radio announcer in 'Good Morning, Vietnam'. Sadly, they are few and far between.

Personal tuition. This, again, totally depends on the quality of the teacher. If, however, you can combine this with falling in love you are home and hosed.

Total immersion commercial courses. In these, for a price, you live and breathe the language all day and everyday for a period of, typically, four weeks. I have yet to find anyone who used these immersion courses and retained a serious competency in any language although I was ever ready to be convinced.

The Gruneberg system of LinkWords. This allows you to build up a vocabulary of about 400 words a week. I tested this with Spanish and found it works extremely well. The basis is to find a mental picture which recalls a word in the most ridiculous manner possible. That for a waiter which is *camerero* in Spanish you think of a waiter with a camera around his neck—probably with a telescopic lens attached. You fix this quite daft mental picture in your brain for about 15 seconds. The same can be done with any word. A cow using a vacuum cleaner in a field reminds you the word for cow is *vaca*. A dog pirouettes in a tutu and that image gives you the association that the word is *perro*. And so on.

There are drawbacks to this system, which is merely a development of an age old method of recall practised by the ancient Greeks: it does not teach pronunciation; it does not teach grammar; it does not work with tonal languages such as Cantonese. On the other hand it does teach complete sentences and more than any other it gives a very quick basic understanding.

The man behind LinkWords is Michael Gruneberg who is at the University of Wales in Swansea. So far the system has not had the success it deserves but in Britain, at least, it seems finally to be making a breakthrough. The system is set out in a series of LinkWord Books published by Corgi and distributed in Australia by Transworld Publishers. These books are frequently out of print and finding one is a hit and miss affair.

One thing I promise you. If you suspend your disbelief and try the system carefully you will find that you will be able to build up a vocabulary of 400 words a week.

Language tapes and records. These are an ideal supplementary way of learning the language and getting the pronunciation roughly right. There is a wide range to choose from with Linguaphone being the oldest and best known. The best I have ever heard have come from the United States government and are basically used for the government's foreign service personnel. There is no copyright in these lessons and you often see them advertised as 'Learn to speak a language the way a diplomat does . . . '

These lessons work if you persevere. The Holborn Library in London, which stocks tapes and records teaching everything from Afrikaans to Welsh, recommends one hour a day for 12 weeks to give a solid grounding. From experience I can say that this will work even better if it is split into two half hour sessions. The first should be just before breakfast and the second just before lunch. Combine these systems with the Gruneberg LinkWord method and you are in with a fighting chance. But only if you persevere. Here we come to the nub of the problem—motivation.

There is little point in trying to learn a language unless you are going to use it in the near future. There seems to me to be little joy in learning a language because, like Everest, it is there. If you are going abroad on holiday or on business being able to speak some of the language of the country you are visiting is a good thing. It will heighten your enjoyment and make your stay much more enjoyable.

Ireland and the language problem

In some countries language is not a problem. Take Ireland where the Irish have laid siege on the English language, stormed the ramparts and made it their own.

They are riotously drunk with the language. Ready at the suggestion of a glass of Guinness to talk from now until then. Able to talk on any subject in the world—and talk entertainingly. Never held back by the narrowness of the truth in time, place or event. A people who love the language. This is what I wrote after my last visit to that talk-mad country.

I will arise and go now, and go to Ireland. For although, it is true, some Australians visit that green and pleasant land, too many miss it and its myriad delights. Ireland of the thousand welcomes, Ireland of the Sorrows, Ireland of a thousand shades of green. I fly in from Gatwick Airport on DanAir and as I have paid my own fare I am free to say that it seems a first-rate commuter airline and the staff are friendly and willing.

At Dublin Airport, I realise I have arrived when I read all the signs which are first in Gaelic, then in English. The taxi-driver is to drive me to my hotel and there is no way he is going to let me speak for he wants to tell me about this old feller out in Donegal, '...which is a lovely place, who was a bachelor and he died and the roof fell in on his cottage and they stuffed his suit with straw and put on a straw head and his little, funny, gold spectacles on that head and, dear God, I looked through the window for the curtains were, you know, partly open, and I saw him and it was a terrible fright I had—I wished I had had a whisky with me for sure'.

It is not just the taxi-driver who has had the terrible fright. I am having the terrible fright, because he is looking at me to make sure I am listening. And making little pantomime gestures with both hands. And all the while we are tacking—the only word—tacking our way through the Dublin traffic.

Arrive at the Shelbourne Hotel, the only place to stay in Dublin—it has been since 1875—and I am welcomed like an old friend. The chief porter, who is a bishop at the very least, has my case taken to my room. Room? Rooms. Two double beds in the bedroom. A lounge. A bathroom large enough and equipped for a Victorian orgy. Two television sets—ten channels on each, all awful.

Unpack and then downstairs into the briskness of the morning and turn right and then down Grafton Street, which is now, thank God, a pedestrian mall. Past the lascivious statue of Molly Malone created in the Penthouse school of sculpture. Give a little snicker, everyone else does.

Now into the yard of Trinity, that great university of Dublin, and across the feet-aching cobblestones and into the library. This is the single largest room for books in the world. There is the glory of The Book of Kells, with a new page being turned over every day. It is important we start with books, for Dublin is, above all else, a literary city. A city that produced George

Bernard Shaw, Jack and W.B.Yeats, J.M.Synge, Sean O'Casey, Brendan Behan and, above all, James Joyce who put the Irish mad intoxication with the English language on to paper.

Go out and head for St Patrick's and it was here, here, that Handel's *Messiah* was first performed in public and it is in this cathedral that Jonathan Swift lies buried, where 'savage indignation can no longer gnaw his heart'.

Return past Marsh's Library, where some of the books are in chains—the library where Dean Swift worked, a man with acid on his tongue and marshmallow for a heart. As he walked the streets of Dublin, he carried loose cash in his pockets to give to the poor who unreservedly loved the man. As do I.

Back into the town past a flower shop called Molly Blooms. Oh, Joyce, what sins are committed in your name ! Lunchtime approaches and, like almost every other Dubliner, we automatically think of Bewley's Oriental Coffee Shop, which is as essential as air to the life in Dublin. And although some damned vandal has done away with the snugs and partitions, it still has the life, the pace, the juice of Dublin. Dublin is not, in any sense of the word, a dry town.

Let us now discuss what is for me one of Dublin's principal attractions: the pubs. Being a newspaperman, I naturally gravitate towards two pubs in that great city on the Liffey—Doheny and Nesbitt's in Lower Baggot Street, and Murphy's, which is behind the offices of *The Irish Independent*. Nesbitt's, to give it the name it is generally known by, has a snug—a sort of small room—at one end and the bar is partitioned in the classic Dublin style, so that a man has something to lean on.

The ceiling is a deep brown and crimson, which is a decorator colour the like of which I have seen nowhere else in the world. I asked the barman how the effect was achieved. He said: 'First you take 200 years of cigarette smoke . . . ' It is not mentioned by James Joyce in any of his works, but the feeling, the authentic feeling, is there. (Read *Ulysses* and you will sense that Leopold Bloom would have approved.)

Most Dubliners will argue at length as to which pub has the best Guinness on tap. (Other beers are not discussed.) The general consensus among journalists is that the best glass of Guinness is served in Murphy's, the other journos' pub. In this, they are wrong. The best Guinness in Dublin is, beyond debate and beyond peradventure, served in the Guinness brewery, which provides tours and a sample of the stuff. This is the Guinness of perfection.

Another pub of which I have the fondest memories—indeed, I was there last night, if I recall correctly—is O'Donoghue's, which is across the road from Nesbitt's. This is where Joyce's Dubliners started and it is a true singing pub. But it is much more than that, for the musicians who sing and play there are of an amazingly high professional standard. As I understand it, they are mainly amateurs—which is surprising.

McDaid's, in Harry Street, has had a slightly unfortunate history. It was, for many years, the literary pub. The mad Irish writers, Paddy Kavanagh, Brendan Behan and Brian O'Nolan, drank, fought and feuded here. Their language was colourful, wonderful, dreadful. When Behan died of the demon grog in 1964, O'Nolan wrote: 'He excelled in language and was a total master of bad language. I have never heard the like of it.' Brendan, who was a house painter by training, once painted the gents' for two pints of Guinness. The landlord of the day recalls: 'Brendan came in and offered to paint the gents' jacks for a couple of pints, which he did, and very well, too.' Those glorious days are past and a younger, trendier set—the culchies in Dublin slang—has taken over. But have a glass of stout there for the ghosts of writers past. I always do, when I am in Dublin.

Another pub with a great literary tradition—and serving a very fair glass of Guinness—is Mulligan's, in Poolbeg Street. There has been a pub there of sorts since 1782, but Mulligan's as we know it dates from the end of the last century. It was in this very pub that, in *Dubliners*, James Joyce explains: '...they went round to Mulligan's. They went into the parlour at the back and O'Halloran ordered small hot specials all round'.

In *Ulysses*, James Joyce wrote: 'He entered Davy Byrne's. Moral pub. He doesn't chat. Stands a drink now and then'. And, this afternoon as ever was, I go into Davy Byrne's. Sadly the pub Joyce described has changed. And not for the better. Leopold Bloom said: 'Nice quiet bar. Nice piece of wood in that counter. Like the way it curves there.' Never more. Now it has been taken over by the culchies and James Joyce sneers for ever from a mural.

Finally, The Brazen Head, which is the oldest pub in Dublin

but not, despite claims to the contrary, the oldest pub in Ireland. (That title goes to Grace Neill's Bar in Donaghadee in County Down, which has been going since 1611.) It is the sort of pub you should visit, just the once, to say you have been there. And the Guinness isn't half bad.

This evening, we will go to the play and to the music, and then to more music, for this is Dublin and there is music in the air. A roaring, tearing, swearing, ramping stamping music. At the bar (in homage to William McGonagall, poet and tragedian), I will stand and recite:

'Twas the twenty-eighth day of November,
Outside of the town of Macroom ...'

They will applaud and buy me a round and say, 'Good man, yourself.' For this is an Ireland where, for the visitor, every meal is a feast, every day a holiday.

And God take you for the misery that you are if you don't believe me.

Finally a story about my friend, the Italian publisher Franco Fasani. He speaks fluent English with an Oxford accent. We were standing on the platform at Torino station. An elderly Englishman approached Franco and in a very loud voice and very slowly shouted in Franco's ear, 'Do-you-speak-English?'

Franco could not resist temptation and shrugged his shoulders Italian style, spread his hands and said, 'No.'

The Englishman shouted back, 'Why not?'

7

Pack up your troubles

Kill the poys and the luggage.
William Shakespeare, *Henry IV, iii, 60.*

Travel light and you can sing in the robbers' face.
Juvenal, *Satires, X*

Packing to travel is an art form. And as in all art forms, there are different schools of thought. So far I have discovered four but there may well be more.

Minimalist. This means cutting down to the bare essentials so that you need only one cabin bag which you can carry on the aircraft. My daughter has this down to a fine art and recently toured India for two weeks with one small, leather Gladstone bag that I bought in China many years ago.

The hard case. This refers not to the character of the traveller but to the suitcase used. Almost all flight crews are hard cases. Watch a Qantas crew collect their baggage from the carousel and you will see that it is all medium-sized, hard-sided suitcases with built-in wheels and handles. Sophisticated travellers sneer at this. But who, I ask, would know better?

The suit bag. Many experienced travellers are of the opinion that a well-made suit bag will last for many years and carry everything you could possibly need. A suit bag used as cabin baggage on overseas flights will almost certainly carry every-

thing you need. On domestic flights, because of size restrictions, this is not normally so.

The enlightened traditionalist. This is a traveller who realises that the suitcase acquired for the first Big Trip at the age of 21 will not cover all needs, all future travel. Horses for courses. Differing bags for different occasions. As a matter of sober truth, I have 32 of the damn things. But I was ever the profligate.

There are, indeed, two types of baggage. The type that will stand up to the rigours of overseas travel, but is so heavy it eats up much of your weight allowance, and that which is light and easy to handle and falls apart at inconvenient moments. There is no such thing as ideal baggage. Only that which can be considered not bad.

If you are going on an overseas trip with more than four stopovers, your present baggage probably will not stand up to the strain. Get a new case before you go or you, too, will scatter your dirty laundry across the departure area of Kai Tak airport to the amusement of hordes of Cantonese travellers.

Do not buy expensive name-brand luggage. They are called 'steal-me' cases on the reasoning that if you can afford a genuine Louis Vuitton suitcase you can afford to pack valuables inside. Look instead for something that is anonymous, easily cleaned and light. Don't worry too much about the quality. After a trip with four stopovers it will not have a long life expectancy.

Do not buy any luggage which has built-in or hang-on gimmicks. They invariably fail. As do combination locks and folda-way handles. Zips are also perhaps best avoided. I have had several sad experiences with zippers which have left me physically and mentally scarred. You may well be luckier.

In my experience, there is no rarer animal than the airport porter—an endangered species—and all airport trolleys vanish on the approach of an aircraft. Therefore, a suitcase with wheels is not a bad idea. Some are easy to manoeuvre, some aren't. Test before you buy. Better yet is a folding trolley which most aircrew members use. Oil the wheels before you leave, otherwise you will squeak, squeak, squeak your way around the world.

Clearly identify your luggage with labels and tags, preferably plastic. Paste your name and address and telephone number into the inside lid. Buy a strap-around belt in a bright colour with a difficult buckle. A hard-to-open buckle deters thieves. If you are absolutely dead-set on preventing theft, buy a second-hand suitcase. Tie it together with rope. Paint on the side in white letters, Kushwant Singh, c/o Palm Line, Lagos. No one will steal it. This I promise you.

Having acquired the right baggage, how do you pack it? Three areas of expertise: frequent travellers, airline cabin staff, butlers and valets. Strangely, all seem to come up with the same advice: fold it carefully, pad it well, pack it tight. The definitive authority on packing is Stanley Ager, who was butler to the second and third Lords St Levan. He would pack a suitcase for their lordships for a sea voyage to East Africa. If, on arrival, the clothes were not instantly ready to wear, he felt he had failed. These are heights to which few of us can aspire, but it is something to aim for.

Rules for packing a suitcase for overseas travel

Place on a bed everything you simply have to take, pared down to the bare essentials. Then deduct 50 per cent.

Brush clothes with a clothes brush before you pack them.

Shirts that have been to the laundry should not be unpacked from their laundry wrappings.

Fold clothes on a bed or on a flat table.

Have a pile of tissue paper for padding. It is agreed generally by the experts that you simply cannot do a half-way decent job without using tissue paper. Use tissue paper to line any folds that you make and to separate garments.

Load a suitcase in the following order: Trousers at the bottom, with the crease towards the handle. Heavy or tweed skirts also go at the bottom. Jackets are packed next. It depends on the length of the jacket and the size of the case. In a very large suitcase you can place them with the collar facing the handle and then the jacket folded in with one centre crease. If this is not possible, lay it lengthwise across the case. Make sure the collar side faces towards the centre of the case, rather than being pressed to one side.

Heavy dresses should be laid towards the bottom of the case with the front facing upwards. Wrap socks around shoes, so that the heels do not damage other goods, before wrapping them in plastic. Fold ties into their own folder of tissue paper. Use socks, gloves, handkerchiefs to fill the spaces.

When you have finished packing try closing the case. It should be as tight a fit as possible without needing excessive force. If it is too loosely packed, lay sheets of tissue paper on top to fill the gap. Many experienced travellers lay a collapsible carry-all on the top for the inevitable excess of baggage on the return journey.

If you are using a hanging bag do not believe that your clothes will, as a result, emerge unwrinkled and wearable. They will not, unless you take special care. The best way to load is with the bag laid flat, not hanging up. Place the shoes in plastic bags, one at each corner, so that they remain at the top when the bag is folded. Make sure the heels are in the corners with the toes pointing towards the handle. Hang the trousers with two folds so that you do not have a single fold across the knee. Do not fasten the jacket, but close it so that one side is about a third of the way across. Fold the sleeves up at the elbow, then pack other garments on top to hold in place.

Unpack both suitcases and hanging bags, completely as soon as you arrive. If there are any wrinkles, hang your clothes on the shower rail and run a very hot bath. Take the plug out and leave the hot tap running. It takes less than an hour to steam the wrinkles out.

Other packing tips

Bottles leak, powder spreads, creams escape and make too much of themselves. The only way that you can be sure that these dread happenings are not among your travel memoirs is to keep all your toiletries in a zip up plastic bag that you have tested for air tightness. Try never to carry any glass bottles. Decant into small plastic holders wherever possible. Always carry a large bar of soap. The little tablets issued in most hotels are not suitable for the cleansing of grown-up bodies. In your toilet kit carry four Alka-Seltzer, four Enos and a card of Panadol—all in foil packages. In your cabin baggage, carry an emergency set of underwear. You never know when it will come in useful.

Carry a spare bag. For a trip in excess of 10 days, put a folding bag on the top of your baggage. You will need it.

Put straps on everything. Locks burst, zips break—always at the most inconvenient moment. Straps will keep your baggage in one piece. I use the webbing straps made in China which are as tough as old boots and easy to cinch tight and the very devil to undo. This gives me an extra feeling of security because thieves hate straps which are difficult to cut, hard to undo.

Label with care and put on distinguishing marks. When the airline mislays your baggage—and this happens less often than you would possibly believe—you will almost always get it back if it is labelled. That means a label inside the case with your name and address and telephone contact number most clearly stated. And labelled twice on the outside. Once with a strap-on tag which must be robust and extremely legible. Once with a stick-on label—ditto.

Make your luggage look different. Even if you only bind the handle with bright tape, make sure your baggage is easy to recognise. This will not help in the recovery of your lost case—airlines only telex the style of suitcase to the last destination, not descriptions. But it will help you to spot your case as it comes off the carousel.

Pack your dirty clothes as carefully as you did your clean clothes. If you do not, your suitcase will become over-full and you will strain it and yourself as you close it. Crumpled clothes take up a third more space than neatly folded clothes.

Always carry Araldite with you. This wonder glue will get

you out of trouble when your suitcase starts to break apart after the constant and unkind attentions of the baggage handlers of the world.

Excess baggage

Once upon a time an Australian traveller was asked what his wife was buying on her first trip to the Orient. He replied, sadly, 'Hong Kong'. Which brings us to the problem of excess baggage and what to do about it.

One system which has much to recommend it is to send small parcels of purchases from each port of call. If you don't mind waiting then you can send them sea mail, which makes the cost comparatively inexpensive and the risks of non-arrival—from our experience—minimal. If time is more critical then you can send them by air mail, although this is quite considerably more expensive.

What you must try to avoid at all costs is being stung for excess baggage at the airport. Airports and airlines vary in their attitudes (Hong Kong is particularly tough, Melbourne fairly relaxed) but you can work on the basis that if your luggage is 5 per cent over the allowed weight you are running a very large risk of being charged at excess baggage rates.

Hong Kong airport has a special counter near the passenger check-in to deal with unaccompanied baggage but, as far as we can ascertain, they are the shining exception. Even so you have to be there three hours before your flight departure time for your baggage to have a chance of flying on the same aircraft as you, and this is in no way guaranteed.

Excess baggage rates are worked on the basis of 1 per cent of the First Class full fare (not the Apex rate or any reduced fare) per kilo and this can soon add up to a horrendous amount, even when airline staff are trying their best to be helpful and minimise the cost.

Note carefully that these rules do not apply worldwide.

The limitations on what you carry to and from the Americas are different. Instead of a weight allowance you are allowed two pieces of baggage. The maximum sizes of the baggage are set down, which means no steamer trunks. Anything over this quota of luggage must be sent either as:

1. 'Excess': Here the rate is reasonable—for example, $US86 per piece Sydney–Los Angeles–or

2. 'Cargo': $US9.37 per kilo Sydney–Los Angeles. Depending on the weight of the luggage, it may well be cheaper to send it 'excess' charged on the piece rate. To avoid this surcharge imposition, consider the possibilities of unaccompanied baggage (baggage sent as cargo) which is available in certain parts of the world.

The prices are relatively reasonable. Usually, unaccompanied baggage is sent at 50 per cent of the normal cargo rate with a minimum charge of 10 kilos.

For example from Sydney to London the normal cargo rate at the time of going to press is $11.69, the unaccompanied baggage rate is $5.85

There are a few simple rules.

1. You must have a ticket for travel which must be produced when you deposit your luggage. The baggage can be sent to any destination listed on that ticket. It can be sent as unaccompanied baggage with one IATA airline even if you are travelling with another IATA airline.

2. Unaccompanied baggage must be sent before or on the day of departure, i.e. baggage can't be sent after your departure. If you want to make sure it will arrive at your destination before or by the time that you do, you should send it a few days before you travel.

3. Unaccompanied baggage is regarded as 'cargo' and must usually be sent from the cargo office at the airport (not from the check-in desk) which has an earlier closing time on a flight—typically three hours before departure—than for ordinary passengers' baggage.

4. According to the regulations in the 'Air Cargo Tariff' book, subscribed to by all major airlines, unaccompanied baggage (baggage shipped as cargo) shall consist of only personal clothes and articles (including portable musical instruments, portable typewriters and portable sports equipment but excluding machinery, machine or spare parts, money, securities, jewellery, watches, plated ware, furs, films, cameras, tickets, documents, liquors, perfumes, articles of household furnishing, merchandise and salesman's samples).

Where unaccompanied baggage is particularly useful is when

it is used to send large quantities of books—which are extremely heavy for their bulk.

Unaccompanied baggage can be sent via the airline office or their cargo agent, which is normally simpler than lugging it to the airport and then finding the cargo office which is frequently hidden out of the way.

There is no such thing as 'unaccompanied baggage' in domestic travel within Australia. The baggage allowance for travel is one piece per person in economy class and two pieces in first class. The pieces have to conform to certain measurements. Anything over this may be sent either as excess or cargo:

1. Excess: charged per piece in the same way as the American system. Examples: $12 Sydney–Perth, and $5 Sydney–Melbourne. The luggage travels on the flight with the person. The rate however changes once a person has three or more pieces of excess luggage. If a person has four pieces of excess, the first two will be charged at the flat rate, whilst for the third and fourth the rate is trebled.

2. For cargo, a base rate is charged plus a rate for each kilogram. Two different prices quoted were: company A (overnight to Melbourne), $46 base rate plus $8.79 a kilogram; (overnight to Perth) $46.97 a kilogram plus $46 base rate. Company B (overnight to Melbourne), $34 base rate plus $6.10 a kilogram; (overnight to Perth) $23 a kilogram plus $34 base rate.

The rules, as you can see, are not uncomplicated but the savings make the exercise well worth while. Especially if you can plan in advance and have the unaccompanied baggage accompany you on the same aircraft.

8

On taking pictures

As far as I knew, he had never taken a photograph before, and the summit of Everest was hardly the place to show him.

Sir Edmund Hillary on the photographic expertise of Tenzing Norgay

The modern pantheist not only sees the god in everything, he takes photographs of it.

D. H. Lawrence, *St Mawr*

When you go on holiday or a trip, you should take a camera and take pictures. If you follow some simple rules, you will take better pictures. No one is suggesting you will thus become a Cartier Bresson nor yet a Richard Avedon, but your pictures will be better.

Be careful where you buy your film. If possible use a chemist or photographic shop that looks busy. Film gets stale and can be badly affected by heat. It needs intelligent storage. This is not normally available at a kiosk in the park with two packages in the window. If you are going abroad consider buying all the film at a duty-free shop in Sydney before you leave. In some countries in Asia the state of the film when it is sold is less than good. Take enough film plus 25 per cent. You will, beyond peradventure, use it.

On overseas trips do not let your film be X-rayed no matter

what the sign says or what the polite security person tells you. Some machines are more damaging than others. Damage to film by X-rays is cumulative. Every time the film goes through a machine it deteriorates. X-ray proof packages for holding film are normally not much chop because, in many airports, when security sees such an opaque package on the screen they turn up the strength so that the contents are revealed. This is not good for film. Keep your film in your hand baggage and ask for it not to be X-rayed. Be polite but firm.

Do not take your camera from an air-conditioned car or room into the open and immediately start taking pictures. Depending on the humidity you will get condensation on all glass surfaces to a greater or lesser degree. Wiping does not fix the problem. It normally takes half an hour or so for everything to return to normal.

Insure all your equipment. Carry with you a photocopy of the original sales slip and guarantee form. This will prevent hassles at the customs.

Do not use a steal-me bag or case. Any bag that looks as though it contains camera gear is a magnet for naughty persons. Any bag that has Hasselblad or Nikon on the side has a short life expectancy. I use a canvas bag mendaciously marked Mendoza—Paris. No one wants to steal that.

Mark all your equipment so that it can be identified. Keep a list of all the numbers. If your gear is nicked and then recovered this will help convince the constabulary that it is rightfully yours. The fewer lenses you take the more you will enjoy your holiday and the better the pictures will be. The number of times you will need to use a telescopic lens are less than you think. If you have a zoom lens which starts from mild wide-angle and then zooms up to, say, 180 mm you are in clover. Nothing is more daunting than lugging around large and heavy camera equipment and then not using it.

A flash is extremely handy for using on sunny days as a fill-in to avoid those desperate dark shadows that obliterate people's faces. For overseas trips, if possible, use one with replaceable, as opposed to rechargeable, batteries. The electricity systems outside Australia can be weird and wonderful. In the Philippines you may find 121 volt and 240 volt in the same room.

Do not save your memories on a new camera. If you buy a new camera, run a test roll through it first. Finding out that the automatic exposure does not work after having shot 20 rolls of film is not a serendipitous experience.

Do not take a tripod with you as it will get in the way and become a nuisance. Instead use any inanimate object—a wall, a post, your partner—to steady you when taking long exposure shots.

Beaches ruin cameras. The sand gets in, the salt spray damages the lens and worse things I could mention. If you must take a camera to the beach, keep it in a separate plastic bag and never put it down on the sand. Or there will be tears before tea-time.

Carry your camera with you. There is little point in leaving it in the hotel bedroom while you go out for a walk. For that is the time, I promise you, that you will have a picture-taking opportunity that will never come your way again. If you are bothering to use a camera, make sure it is constantly available. Those are the basic rules to stop you getting into trouble.

Now for taking the pictures

Special circumstances need special techniques. For example, if you are taking photographs from an aircraft, make sure that no part of the camera or your upper body is in contact with the window. The vibrations will ruin the shot. Sit up, clamp your elbows to your side. Do not photograph with the lens at perfect right angles to the window. Angle slightly. This way you will avoid reflections.

At night, know the range of your flash unit. As the sign says, it is shorter than you think. There is nothing sadder than seeing amateur photographers snapping away at the lights of Hong Kong, some twelve kilometres distant, and using a flash gun to lighten the scene. Most flashes do not carry twelve kilometres. Few will have any effect at twelve metres.

If you want to record the scenic wonders of a place, whether it be Byron Bay or Singapore, cheat. This is the way you do it. Buy a complete set of picture postcards. The photographers who took them live in the area, are professionals and know the best angles. Go forth and imitate them. Once you have got a duplicate shot, use your imagination, initiative and artistic style, and take others. I have used this technique to cover Singapore for an audio visual. It took two days. I was complimented on my artistic skill and integrity.

People are more interesting than scenery. Always try to get a figure into your pictures, even if it is only to give a sense of scale. The most beautiful landscape can look sadly flat without humans to give proportion.

What camera to use?

Most modern cameras are little marvels and will do everything except select the scene for you. Automatic exposure and, more and more, automatic focusing. For the record, I use Canon EOS cameras because they are idiot-proof, take professional quality pictures and are the right price. I use a zoom which goes from 50 mm to 200 mm and this covers pretty much everything I will need to photograph. Even that I find sometimes too heavy and so I also carry a Minox, which is the size of a packet of cigarettes and has only a single lens. With that single camera I once did a major picture story for Cathay Pacific on China. No one knew that I had used only the one small camera. The results were, technically, superb.

Final rule. Make sure the little piece of glass points towards the eye, the big piece of glass towards the subject and the lens cap is off before pressing the button.

9

Keeping in touch

As cold waters to a thirsty soul, so is good news from a far country.
The Bible, *Proverbs*, 25:25

On your own small island in the Pacific or climbing a mountain in the Himalayas, sailing the Mediterranean or slogging through the jungles of Papua New Guinea—wherever you are in the world (just about) you can pick up an English-speaking radio station. This is the miracle of shortwave radio.

Australia's own shortwave radio station, Radio Australia, has more than 100 million listeners every day. Like most of the other international broadcasters, Radio Australia transmits in several different languages. English predominates, though, and if you have the booklet detailing the times and frequencies Radio Australia broadcasts to the various parts of the world, tuning in shouldn't be a problem. It is a comfort to hear 'This is Radio Australia, the overseas service of the ABC', when you are swatting at malaria-ridden mosquitoes in darkest Africa.

If, perchance, you cannot pick up Radio Australia, there is always the BBC Overseas Service, famous for the words 'This is London calling'. Failing the BBC, the Voice of America blankets most of the world with its broadcasts.

Most of the major countries in the world, in fact, operate international shortwave broadcasting stations. Shortwave transmissions are bounced off the ionosphere at such an angle

that, although most of NSW misses out on Radio Australia broadcasts much of the rest of the world receives it loud and clear.

You do not have to be a radio ham to pick up shortwave broadcasts. Those huge bulky contraptions with earphones and microphones—á la Flying Doctors—are transceivers. These are not necessary unless you want to transmit and receive. All a listener needs is a receiver which need not be much bigger, nor more expensive, than the standard transistor radio. Indeed, you probably have a radio already that will fit the bill. Many people have radios with SW bands and have no idea of their function. Radios with shortwave bands can be picked up at department stores. (Prices range from around $70 to $400.)

If you are buying one, a specialty shop is probably the best bet. Some shops provide a booklet with every radio listing all the important dial settings (the frequencies) for most of the major shortwave stations in the world. So apart from listening in English you can polish up your French or German as well.

How good is the reception? It depends very much on where you are, the time of day and the state of the weather. Although short waves can reach parts the longer waves cannot they can still be blocked by steel and concrete constructions. In some modern hotels where the structure becomes, effectively, a device known as a Faraday cage blocking out signals, reception can be difficult. The solution is to listen in the open air.

Incidentally, never try use your radio on an aircraft. This is a no-no as it might interfere with the navigation equipment.

Shortwave reception always seems to me to be better at night. This may be because there are fewer transmission stations competing for the air waves.

During bad weather and strong sunspot activity your radio can give you a lot of snap, crackle and pop. The more sophisticated the set the better the suppression of these unwanted noises. You will frequently find you can improve the quality of reception by turning the wireless around on its axis.

Is it worthwhile? Earlier this year on the banks of the Mekong River opposite Laos it was possible to find out the scores in the Rugby League final.

10

Joining the club

Please accept my resignation. I don't want to belong to any club that will accept me as a member.

Allegedly by Groucho Marx when resigning from the Friar's Club in Hollywood.

Airlines love frequent travellers. They pay full fare, are more travel savvy, and create fewer problems than other passengers. And they are loyal to a fault. What more can be asked of a consumer? As a result, the airlines of the world woo the frequent traveller with an undisguised ardour. The principal expression they give to their requited love is membership of a frequent travellers' club. Membership is offered often without charge to those who plight their troth and prove their continuing loyalty with ticket stubs. What does membership of these clubs mean? Most frequent-flyer programs offer the following benefits:

The frequent traveller is immortalised on a computer. Preferences are recorded and automatically applied as soon as the booking is made. This works very well. If you prefer a window seat, once the computer is told, you will always be assigned one.

Baggage is tagged so that, in theory, at least, it comes off the aircraft first. In the past year or so it has begun to work efficiently.

A special baggage allowance sees to it that under normal

circumstances you don't have to pay excess.

In many cases, perhaps most cases, special lounges are provided at principal airports so that you can have some peace and quiet.

Most frequent travellers' clubs offer discounts at hotels and car-hire companies. Generally, this is not worth much because better discounts can be arranged on the spot.

In theory, a frequent traveller will be first in the queue for an upgrade from one class to another. In practice, the captain's spouse has priority, followed by airline staff and relatives of the airline's marketing manager.

Membership of these frequent travellers' clubs is normally either free or available for a nominal charge. All you have to do is prove you have flown the requisite number of kilometres. In the US and Australia, all domestic frequent flyers' clubs charge for membership—in the US because of legal constraints and in Australia because of sheer numbers. Charging a substantial fee ensures the system is not totally flooded. What follows is not a comprehensive guide to all the frequent travellers' clubs, more a selective overview.

Domestic

Ansett Golden Wing The game to beat. Tom Dery, the general marketing manager of Ansett, made no secret of the fact that he wanted the best inflight club in the world. The club has eleven lounges, which provide light refreshments, a place to sit and work and a competent reception desk that sorts out bookings. As well, there is valet car parking, a lost-luggage service and reciprocal rights with other inflight clubs, including Cathay Pacific, British Airways and American Airlines. Note that you do not need to be flying to use the lounge. Membership costs $335 for the first year and $185 a year after that. You can buy life membership for $1850, which may turn out to be a serious bargain depending where you stand in the longevity stakes. Entry into the lounges is restricted to genuine members and first-class passengers. Ansett also offers discounted spouse membership. Wife or husband can have their own membership card for $110 a year. Spouse life membership is $1100.

Australian Airlines Flight Deck Club Not as brashly commercial as Golden Wing and possibly even more civilised. It has ten lounges and reciprocal rights with British Airways, United Airlines, Air New Zealand, Canadian Pacific and North West Orient. Extra jollies: free postage for your mail in Australia, cashing facilities for personal cheques up to $100 when you are desperate and showers in the washroom. Annual membership is $200 a year and life membership is $1500.

On Australian Airlines, spouse membership costs $50 a year; spouse life membership is $500. If you travel frequently by air in Australia, you should join one of these two clubs.

Overseas

Note that qualification mileage quoted here is for economy class. On most airlines, business class gives you 30 per cent weighting, while for first class it is 50 per cent or more.

Cathay Pacific Marco Polo The first frequent travellers' flight club in Asia. Started by Keith Sillett, the man most responsible for taking Cathay Pacific from Mickey Mouse to great. Now there are 29 lounges in airports around the world.

To join, you have to travel 35 000 km in twelve months. There is also gold membership available at 50 000 km and a diamond membership at an amazing 300 000 km or roughly nine return trips a year to Europe in economy. Don't think there are no such creatures as diamond members. They exist. Members are fanatical supporters of the airline and wear the club tie.

Qantas Frequent Travellers' Club It costs $25 to become an associate member. Full membership is 70 000 km—about two-and-a-bit return tickets to Europe or 12 sectors. All of the usual benefits with an extra 10 kg baggage allowance. However, you cannot use their lounges if you hold an economy ticket due to pressure of space, but Qantas is working on the problem.

Air New Zealand Frequent Flyers' Club Qualification is four short or two long international trips a year. Check-in at the first-class counters at fifteen airports. Access to sixteen first-class airport lounges. Travel insurance for a single annual premium of $225.

Singapore Airlines Priority Passenger Service You must fly 60 000 km or fifteen flight sectors a year. All the usual benefits—eighteen Silver Kris lounges, check-in at business class, priority wait list, plus an amazing emergency service which takes care of you should you become ill in a foreign land. This, I think, is unique.

Philippines Mabuhay Club Membership qualification is 48 000 km. Usual benefits: four lounges, more planned, use of Philippine Airlines offices world-wide as a messaging service, plus a free mileage program that offers 20 per cent of tickets bought as future free travel.

Lufthansa Frequent Traveller Service Offers membership when you have completed two return flights to Europe in one year. Usual benefits as well as first-class free baggage allowance and expert travel advice from the team of Lufthansa sales consultants.

Others

There are many more frequent travellers' clubs—British Airways, United Airlines and others. I am a life member of Pan Am's Clipper Club and got my money's worth in the first twelve months. Now I use it as an United Airlines frequent travellers' card.

This is a sad example of how airlines can change the rules to their own benefit and the detriment of the club member. Recently in Miami airport I made use of the Clipper lounge. There was a charge of $US3 for a scotch. All that was free was coffee.The person behind the bar had a glass full of dollar gratuities. When I become a life-time member in 1972 the drinks in all clipper lounges were free. If I had known I would be charged $US3 a drink I probably would never have joined.

Neverthe less, any traveller who flies frequently should join one of these clubs. The lounges are islands of peace and sanity in the oceans of madness that make up modern airports.

11

Travelling by train

God! I will pack, and take a train,
And get me to England once again!

Rupert Brooke

Mussolini and my mother had something in common. They could both make trains run on time. Where I was born the railway system was the Great Western Railway. It was all steam, then. Before the start of any journey my mother would hobble down to the front of the train—she was an arthritic—and summon the driver with a gnarled finger. She would say 'I have a very important appointment at the end of this journey and I would be pleased if you got there on time'. No train she rode arrived late. The record was a Cardiff to London express that arrived at Paddington Station 38 minutes early.

It was from my mother that I learned that trains could be punctual conveyances. It was from the poet, Edward Thomas, that I learned about the magic of trains.

> Yes, I remember Adlestrop—
> The name—because one afternoon
> Of heat the express-train drew up there
> Unwontedly. It was late June.
> The steam hissed. Someone cleared his throat.
> No-one left and no-one came
> On the bare platform...

No poem ever better evoked for me memories of train journeys in England in the steam age. Now, from preference, wherever I go, I travel by train. I have found, as countless travellers have found before me, that trains are more comfortable, cheaper and often a lot faster than aircraft. Trains take you from city centre to city centre, aircraft do not. Trains do not need air traffic controllers. In a train you can move around, walk up and down, swap seats, watch the ever changing scenery. This is not easy in an overcrowded 747.

Trains can be divided into two or three main groups. There are those that you ride for the sheer pleasure of travel. At one end there is the Venice–Simplon Orient Express. At the other, the Tal-y-llyn narrow gauge wandering around the hills of Wales. There are those that you ride to get somewhere with speed, ease and efficiency. The two best examples of this type are the TGV (Train à Grande Vitesse) in France and the Bullet trains in Japan.

There is, I believe, a third category which combines these first two. That is trains that you use as transport but that are also sheer pleasure. The example that springs to mind is the Thai Railways special. This runs from Bangkok down to Hat Yai, over the Thai-Malay border to Butterworth and then on down to Singapore.

The Orient Express is a wondrous example of travel for its own sake. You board in Venice at a civilised time in the morning and then proceed—travel is not a stately enough word—through Innsbruck, Paris, Boulogne and arrive at London Victoria late in the evening of the following day. During that time you will have eaten meals to roughly Michelin one-star standard, slept in an air-conditioned cabin with single beds and ridden in one of the great Pullman carriages. All in a grand tradition which nowadays hardly exists anywhere else. You will, of course, dress up to the standards of the train. To do otherwise would lack style.

The price of this total travel experience is about $1600. The only extras are wine and tips. All of which you, like me, may find remarkably cheap for the trip of a lifetime.

The only drawback that I can see in riding this splendid train is that one romantic aspect of train travel is ill-catered for by those single bunks. I have it on good authority that the Orient Express has only been inadvertently stopped once in its history. This happened as it was passing through Switzerland. When the train halted the driver and the guard walked back down the train checking each of the 17 carriages. In the last carriage they found a young Australian honeymooning couple who were still celebrating their nuptials in traditional style in the top bunk. To avoid falling from grace, as it were, the young lady was hanging on for dear life to the communication cord.

The same pleasure in travel for its own sake—we are back to talking about trains again—exists with the narrow gauge railways of the world. We have our own Zig Zag just before you come down from the Blue Mountains to Lithgow. If you have not tried this splendid journey you have missed out.

In Britain, especially in Wales, the place is a-crawl with narrow gauge railways run by mad-keen enthusiasts. The best known in Wales is the Tal-y-llyn railway which was originally opened in 1865 and restored by enthusiasts in 1951. It has run continuously ever since. You ride in the oldest passenger coaches in the world still in service. The railway winds its way through Welsh countryside until it ends up at the Tywyn terminus where there is a narrow gauge museum.

The most famous in England is the Bluebell line in the southeast. This is currently the subject of a major scandal. The operating committee has suggested that diesel engines be used for shunting operations in the marshalling yard. For dyed-in-the-wool steam enthusiasts this is akin to spitting in the Bible. 'Outraged' of Tunbridge Wells and 'Old Puffer' of Worthing and thousands of others have written letters of screaming protest.

As, indeed, they should.

All of that is travelling by train for the sake of it. In Europe one travels by train because it is frequently the most cost-effective way of travelling. That is not to say there are no pleasurable journeys. There are many. But the main intent is to use the train as a means of transport.

I have come to the conclusion that almost anyone visiting Europe for a holiday should seriously consider the Eurail Pass which is available in Australia through Thomas Cook. You should buy this season pass in Australia before you leave.

A couple of caveats. The further south you go in Europe the less desirable the trains, the less pleasant and efficient the service. Britain is only theoretically part of Europe. Its train service, even when it is not strike-bound, is not of the best. Nevertheless, for most intercity travel it beats flying for both speed and economy. That is utilitarian train travel.

Finally there is train travel that combines the romantic with the practical. This reached its height in the United States just after World War II. 'Along steel rails, across cross-ties, I'm on my way back home. The train I ride is the queen of them all, The Streamlined Cannonball'. Now most American trains are run by Amtrak and have lost some of their soul but the names are still there: The Orange Blossom Special; The Twentieth Century Limited; The Atchison, Topeka and the Santa Fé.

The train . . .'moves along like a cannonball, like a star in its heavenly flight'. When you hear that lonesome whistle blow you will realise that trains offer something that no other form of transport can manage.

Mexico

I am sitting on a low wooden bench in the railway station of Ciudad Juarez. There is very little to keep me company except for the flies. The ticket office is shut. I have been travelling almost non-stop for 32 hours. I have not eaten for the last twelve. I am so tired I ache. What, I ask myself, am I doing here? The answer is that I have come to go for a train ride; but such a train ride. Through an area as dramatic as, yes, the Grand Canyon.

I have been to Mexico on three previous occasions and found Acapulco exhilarating, Jalisco exciting and Mexico City a great worry. I know little of the Copper Canyon and the ride from Chihuahua to Los Mochis. I first came across it while reading Fodor's quite excellent guide to Mexico. The book described the train ride as 'the world's most scenic rail ride'. Which is why I have now arrived at the deserted station of Ciudad Juarez.

It used to be that you could fly Qantas direct to Mexico City by way of Tahiti. No longer. Now you must go by way of the United States. Qantas very kindly flew me non-stop to Los Angeles. From there I had to get myself to the Copper Canyon and its amazing railroad.

I came into Mexico by an unorthodox route. I flew by an overnight 'red eye' to El Paso in Texas by way of Las Vegas and Albuquerque. From El Paso I took a taxi to Ciudad Juarez, the sister city of El Paso. Juarez is just across the Rio Grande. Juarez railway station is not jolly. A concrete structure open to the air on one side, like a bomb shelter. Low, dirty, dilapidated benches on which to sit; a lavatory I dare not investigate for the smell would choke a horse; and nothing else. Nothing at all. No soft drink machine. No news stand. Nothing. Except for flies.

This is the lowest point of the trip. As I get on the train that will take me to Chihuahua everything improves dramatically. The six o'clock train for which I buy a first class reserved ticket is of a very high standard. The ticket costs 18 750 pesos which I work out to be around $10. This for a journey of more than 400 kilometres.

The train is nothing like the station. The carriage is blessedly air-conditioned. It is squeaky clean and the seats recline aircraft-style. I laugh aloud with relief. The train goes first through the suburbs, the poor suburbs, of Juarez. Now we are travelling across a flat plain with dry vegetation. Very similar to Australia.

The conductor—immaculately dressed as are all the staff on the train—comes through the train and announces dinner. There are few takers. Foolhardy to the end, I walk through to the dining car and face a pre-set dinner. A small plastic cup of Coca-Cola . A plastic plate with four potato crisps, two Saltine biscuits, a spoonful of cold macaroni, a small portion of shredded dry fish. As a meal this neither inspires nor encourages me.

The train pulls into Chihuahua station. A fleet of taxis, rapacious hawks to a man, lie in ambush. They want 10 000 pesos to take me to a hotel. Brisk haggling gets this down to 6000 pesos.

This hotel, the Exelaris, was once a Hyatt. No longer.

I arrange for a wake-up call at 5.30 am so that I can catch the train to Los Mochis. Out to the station and claim my seat on the Chihuahua–Pacific railway which covers the 640 kilometres to Los Mochis.

I am in the super deluxe Pullman which costs $62 one-way. There are two other classes. First class costs $22 and second, which I do not recommend, costs $11. First class appears to me to be perfectly adequate with airliner-type reclining seats. The Pullman class I am in is much the same as when I came down from El Paso. The train ride down to Los Mochis is one of the great travel bargains of the age. It is the connecting rail link between the United States and the Sea of Cortez.

This stretch of rail was the dream of Albert Owen who envisaged the line a century ago. Envisaging it was one thing, bringing it to reality another. Many attempts were made and all failed. In 1940 the Mexican Government bought the still uncompleted railroad. At each end much work had been completed. In the middle, a 240-kilometre gap crossing the precipitous country; where the Tarahumara Indians live. In the centre was the quite awesome Copper Canyon which had to be skirted.

In 1953 work started and the line completed eight years later. There are 39 bridges and 86 tunnels. The train stops at eleven stations during the ten-hour journey. (The eight o'clock train, which takes an extra two hours, stops at over 50.)

We leave Chihuahua and the scenery is flat, almost Australian, not riveting. Then the train starts climbing in a series of snaking turns to Creel which is a timber town. After Creel we keep climbing and the air turns distinctly brisk. It is two in the afternoon. Just before the Copper Canyon is Divisadero where the train stops for a quarter of an hour. Tarahumara Indians on the platform sell souvenirs to the tourists. This always makes me so sad.

Now on to Copper Canyon. As large as the Grand Canyon but it spreads its impact out through six canyons instead of getting you with one king hit. The scenery is, the only word for it, astounding. Someone once told me of taking a sightseeing flight with the Hallelujah Chorus played as each canyon came into sight. The Chorus is precisely what this trip deserves. Fortissimo. There is, indeed, a God.

As I look out of the train window I can see over there, on the opposite side, another railway going in the opposite direction. What is this railway? Where is it going? It is, of course, the rail that I ride, doubling back on itself to get around the canyon walls.

The track turns, loops, twists, gyrates. The train snaking as it seeks the way to go. The train passes 100 metres above the Chinipas River. From the window I cannot see the bridge. I am suspended in space. I am slightly afflicted by vertigo and sweat and stare in wild surmise. My hands grip knuckle-white. Eventually I relax, get blasé—this is, after all, a ten-hour trip. I start to inspect my fellow passengers, pause to drink a beer, talk to the person sitting next to me. Yet always the scenery drags me back.

It was dark when we got into Los Mochis so that I missed some of the spectacular scenery on the run to the sea. No matter. The next day I arose early again and took the train back to Chihuahua. This time I took the slow train. Mexico is not a place where one wishes to rush things.

Asia

The trains in Asia are something else again.

The train pulls out of Bangkok precisely on time. It is immaculately, squeaky clean. No graffiti. The railway guards in spotless, freshly pressed, light khaki cotton uniforms. Smiling as they help you board.

I sit in a second-class compartment, somewhere between Bangkok and Hat Yai on the Isthmus of Kra, where Thailand snakes down to meet Malaysia. How did this come about? A reader called to ask whether the train journey between Bangkok and Singapore was comfortable, safe, feasible.

I had made part of the journey before. But at a darker and more dangerous time. It was in the fifties and I went with a company of Gurkhas up the Malaysian peninsula to Perak. We boarded the train at Johor Bahru, just across the Causeway from Singapore. The Gurkhas had spent four weeks on patrol in the *ulu*, the deep jungle. They were sweaty, tired and exhausted and they had no interest in a Welsh sergeant who theoretically commanded the guard but spoke no Gurkhali. In the dark of the train, they slumped in their jungle greens, rarely smiled, ignored me.

Later, when the train was stopped by CTs—communist terrorists—I realised once again the virtues of the Gurkha as a soldier. They went into action like a well-oiled, eager machine. The Bren gunner letting off short controlled bursts. The riflemen rolling under the train and returning fire with their jungle short Lee Enfields. The CTs had made an error of judgment and withdrew into the *belukar*, the secondary jungle that grew by the tracks.

That journey took two-and-a-half days. There was no air-conditioning, no bunks, no smiling vendors. Only tired Gurkhas awaiting the next night action. Now I am finding out how this train journey has changed.

We get to Bangkok station in plenty of time. A porter with an immense and awkward baggage cart takes care of our luggage for 50 cents. On platform seven, where the train is standing, up-country boys lie in groups, lethargic in the heat of the height of the Thailand summer with their baggage—cardboard boxes tied with string. On top of the boxes are fighting cocks, metallic shimmers in the light. A young Buddhist in his saffron robe carefully inspects his sandals. Children lie on benches in the heat in boneless sleep.

We are led to our seats on the train. Ultra wide and comfortable. The Thai passenger across the way is rubbing *pak fai yau*, the universal Chinese panacea made from eucalyptus oil, into his forehead. The loudspeaker is quietly playing Thai music, which I find wondrously soothing.

This is not expensive travel. In second class, where we are, the seats are cheap. From Bangkok to Butterworth in Malaysia costs a basic 431 baht, while from Bangkok to Singapore, the fare is 899 baht. That is roughly $A22 and $A45. On top of this are other supplements—50 baht because this is a special express, 70 baht because I have an upper sleeping berth. If I had the lower sleeping berth, it would cost me 100 baht—roughly $5. Work on the basis of 20 baht to the Australian dollar to see how cheap it is.

We are getting off in Hat Yai, which is the stop before Butterworth, and the total fare is under $A30 each. I am travelling second class from choice, because it suits me. Not for financial reasons. We could have gone by bus which is faster and air-conditioned. But dangerous. The buses run video movies and the story is that the drivers like to watch them. (My companion, Bill, a fellow but rival journalist, asks me not to use this because he wants it for his piece. Sure, Bill, sure.)

In theory, this train will stop at Nakom Pathom—the biggest temple, *chedi,* in Thailand—Ratchabiri, Petchaburi, Hua Hin (where they filmed *The Killing Fields*), Chumphon, Surat Thai, Thang Song, Phatabulang and then Hat Yai. A journey which will take 14 hours. Six hours later, it will be in Butterworth in Malaysia.

The listed stations turn out to be those that are thought important, because almost as soon as we move off, we stop again at San Sen and then Bang Sue. Perhaps these are temporary hiccups, for the train is in each station for only two minutes at the most. Still, vendors come through the train selling nuts, magazines and sticky sweets wrapped in plastic.

Sitting opposite me is a Thai girl. (Sitting opposite Bill is an elderly Thai gentleman. Bill offers to swap seats. I refuse.)

She speaks no English, I no Thai. We communicate with smiles and gestures. She, too, is using *pak fai yau* on her temples. She is about nineteen. Her boyfriend, a tall, handsome Thai, has seen her off. She has her hair in a long pigtail and is wearing a thin gold necklace, a gold bracelet, gold earrings and a gold ring. Strangely, she is wearing a thick, brown woollen sweater. Presumably against the chill of the air-conditioning. As soon as she gets to her seat, she slips off her shoes and curls her feet almost as if she were yoga trained. She manages to sleep in this position. Would that I were that limber.

In the first hour of travel, the carriage is swept once and mopped, properly mopped, twice. The train is moving out of the city, across *klongs*—the canals of Thailand—past temples, over traffic-jammed level crossings. The train is not travelling fast. Speed is not a feature of Thai railways. A small black-and-white bird, the size of a rosella, overtakes the train and dives towards the klong. A guard comes through and offers every passenger a cold towel impregnated with scent. The towels are in plastic bags marked 'Prateep Railway Business Company'.

At the side of the permanent way, we keep passing children playing with their kites. Will not the passing train suck the kites to their destruction? Apparently not.

Just after four o'clock an attendant comes through and gives each passenger a large pillow with a spotlessly clean white pillow case. We are passing rice fields, coconut groves, villages, more rice fields. The Orient Express company is considering putting one of its ultra deluxe trains on this run. But that, for my money, does not sound like a real train. Here in second class, I know I am on a rail journey, travelling on a real train. The Orient Express sounds as if it would suit Double Bay yuppies. Not me.

In the middle distance are white birds, like cormorants, in the rice fields. Everything is green and wet and irrigated, although this is just the end of the hot season and the rains will not come until next month.

Later, we come out of the irrigation area and the land is brown and dry. Next month, the rains. As we pass through Ratchburi, the sun starts to lower in the sky. The people in the coach have settled down for the journey. This is middle-class Thailand travelling. Everyone looks prosperous, well-dressed. An army captain walks through the carriage. He smiles at me most pleasantly and greets me with a '*Sawadee kap*.' Such polite people.

The small stations we roll past have small, carefully tended gardens. They remind me of the Great Western Railway of my youth, when stations were the pride and joy of the station master. The only sadness is that the engine in front is diesel, not steam.

As the sun fades, over to the right, we see the most odd shapes of mountains springing round and high from the flat soil of the plain. Right on the horizon, where they are blue with mist, are the mountains of Burma. The rhythm of the train is starting to creep into my consciousness. It is a potent tranquilliser and I sit quiet and enraptured. I do not bother to read. Just make an occasional note. There is, I am sure, such a state as traveller's trance. I manage it very easily when I am travelling long distances. I am still awake, still functioning, but as a somnambulist. It is a very pleasant though slightly odd feeling.

Just after six o'clock, the waiter comes through asking for orders for dinner. I order Tom Yam Gung, a hot soup with shrimps, and the unfortunately named Cow Pat Gung, which is fried rice with shrimps. And to go with it, a large bottle of

Klosters beer. Tables are set up between the seats which lock into position on the wall and floor. Dinner is served just after seven o'clock. I chew on a small green chilli in the soup. An explosion in my mouth. My lips go numb. My nose, my eyes, my ears are watering. I hurl down rice and beer to stop the burning. From across the table, I get an interested glance and a small smile. Not a sniggering smile. A sympathetic smile. The fire abates. Matters return to normal.

After the dinner, plates are cleared away. The cabin attendant comes and starts converting the seats into bunks—upper and lower. By eight o'clock, everyone is in their bunks, presumably asleep. My top deck bunk is supremely comfortable. At the foot, there are three hangers. To my left is a small hanging net bag to hold my valuables. Next to that, a reading light. I am sheltered from the world by pinkish curtains. A warm cocoon of safety.

I wake up at five o'clock as the train comes to a halt. Two hours to Hat Yai. An hour later, the passengers are awake and the attendant comes along and reassembles the bed back into two chairs. My travelling companion has let her hair down. The pigtail has gone. I am brought a cup of instant coffee, powdered milk and two biscuits. Outside, the sky is lightening and, lo, already on the hills, the flags of dawn appear.

The train pulls into Hat Yai station. A strange mixture of Muslim and railway architecture. We have arrived and a taxi will soon take us the 20 km from Hat Yai to Songkhla for $5. I am a contented traveller.

Europe

Anything is possible on a train, a great meal, a binge, a visit from card players, an intrigue, a good night's sleep, and strange monologues framed like Russian short stories.

Paul Theroux, *The Great Railway Bazaar.*

To travel Europe by train, second class, is to be perpetually surrounded by legions of the young and impoverished and unwashed for whom trains are both a means of conveyance and a sleeping apartment. It means rarely setting foot in a hotel. The Grand European Tour is spent in a haze of weariness, a blinking stupor of fatigue and smelly armpits. This is not, I promise you, the way to see Europe. A Eurailpass should be used intelligently.

A Eurailpass entitles you to unlimited train travel within a certain time span. This tempts many people to try and get a lot for not very much. Trying to wring every last centime and sou of value from a Eurailpass is asking for trouble. Trying to visit every one of the 17 countries participating in the Eurail scheme within 14 days is verging on the ridiculous. The budget-minded who attempt this do not savour Europe. It is a case of 'this is Tuesday, so this must be Belgium'. Take it reasonably easy and pace yourself. Then travelling with a Eurailpass makes eminent sense.

Eurail came into existence because Western European railroads had a new and expensive network of inter-city trains that needed riders. The idea was to entice potential passengers from the other side of the Atlantic by offering two months of unlimited second-class travel on any or all of the member rail systems. The first passes were issued in 1959 and 5000 were sold. Later developments included one and three month passes,15-day passes, first-class passes, youth passes and fringe benefits like free ferry and steamer travel. Today, there are several different kinds of Eurailpass. All are non-transferable, offer unlimited travel within the allotted timespan and are mostly non-refundable. Reservations are usually not necessary. The few lines that do require advance bookings are listed in the official timetable.

Eurail passes cannot be bought in Europe—and they must be validated within six months of purchase. It is best to buy your pass here in Australia.

Types of Eurailpass

The standard Eurailpass, which offers first-class travel, is available for different lengths of time from fifteen days to three months.

Eurail Youthpass, only for people aged 26 or under, and only good for second-class travel but a considerable saving in price.

The Eurail Saverpass works for two or more people travelling together for 15 days (except between 1 April and 30 September when at least three people are required). This Saverpass is valid for first-class travel, just like the standard Eurailpass, but at a reduced rate.

The latest development on the Eurail scene is the Flexipass

which is good for a number of days of first-class travel. With the Flexipass, the travelling days can be staggered over a period of time.

To decide whether or not a Eurailpass will prove a worthwhile buy is a difficult task. If you intend to whiz from the Arctic Circle to the Mediterranean, on a whistle-stop tour of Europe, then a Eurailpass is definitely a good idea. For a sampling of the Continent, to decide which countries are worthy of later and more leisurely perusal, Eurailpass cannot be bettered.

For the train buff there is no other way to go. Otherwise, it is worthwhile considering other options, including car hire, flying and point-to-point tickets. The official Eurail brochure says, 'A general rule of thumb is that if your two-week rail travel plans cover 1500 miles (2400 kilometres) or more, the Eurailpass is your best buy; otherwise, consider regular point-to-point tickets'.

Other benefits of travelling by Eurailpass include fewer queues, arriving at train stations that are usually in the centre of the city, rather than airports miles from nowhere, and a relaxing journey. If Britain plays a large part in your travel plans, bear in mind the fact that Britain is a non-participant. For unlimited train travel there you will have to purchase a BritRail pass. (This situation is supposed to change in 1992. Don't hold your breath.) A quick comparison of prices:

- A 15-day Eurailpass—$410;
- A 15-day Eurail Saverpass—$295;
- A 15-day Toyota Corolla rental—$964. (This price, from International Car Travel, does not include fuel, but does allow you to drop the car in a different city.)
- A 15-day tour using aeroplanes—say a round trip, Amsterdam, Munich, Paris, Rome, Naples, Amsterdam. It is necessary to fly a variety of different carriers, as no single airline covers this route. KLM quoted a standard economy fare of $1845. This seems on the high side, but it is well nigh impossible to get excursion fares for this sort of itinerary.

Using Eurail Flexipass

Unlimited travel by train (and sometimes by other means) in seventeen countries for a period ranging from fifteen days to three months, on a pre-paid ticket, makes it easy to travel from

Norway to Portugal or from Ireland to Greece.

Some travellers, determined to have their money's worth, rush madly up and down Europe, practically living on trains. That's all right if you like living on trains. But it's a good idea to get out sometimes and take a look at places along the way. Realising this, the Eurail people introduced Flexipass, which allows unlimited travel on either seven or fifteen days in a two-month period.

This means that you can make your long and medium-length journeys on those days, using your Eurailpass, and stay several days or a week before using your pass again. Buy local day tickets if you want to use trains for short journeys. If you are going to stay within one country all or most of the time, ask your travel agent if that country has a national pass such as France Vacance, Swiss Pass or Germany's DB Tourist Card. A Eurailpass will allow you to spend, say, a fortnight exploring Spain and Portugal, then head for Switzerland.

Switzerland and its neighbours, Germany, Austria, Italy, France, provide wide scope for Eurailpassing. A word of warning: there are many private railways in Switzerland, and they vary as to what passes (if any) they accept. It's always wise to ask. On the plus side, Eurail covers travel by regular ferry services on the principal Swiss lakes, and the ferry on the Rhine between Kreuzlingen and Schaffhausen. (Don't miss the Rhine Falls at Schaffhausen.)

With standard Eurailpass, it's possible to stay in one place for several nights and use your pass for excursions that are all the more enjoyable because you're travelling without luggage. So much the better if you choose a town from which there are trains in several directions.

Japan Rail Pass

Japan's equivalent to the Eurailpass is the Japan Rail Pass. This ticket offers the bearer unlimited travel on JR trains, including the *shinkansen* or 'bullet train'. It cannot be used on railways, ferries and buses owned by other companies. As with the Eurailpass, this ticket is worthwhile only if you intend doing a lot of travelling by rail. It can only be purchased outside Japan by foreign tourists.

The trains in Japan are not covered with graffiti and they do not have seats missing and stuffing ripped out. They are fast, clean, punctual and economical.

If you buy a Japan Rail Pass, do not travel at night. Firstly, because you will miss out on the beautiful Japanese countryside and, secondly, because you will have to pay extra for a sleeper. This can be as much as the price of a good hotel. The long-distance trains have smoking and non-smoking cars and carry dining or buffet cars or both. Also available from vendors on trains and station platforms are bento box lunches, containing local specialty Japanese-style foods or snacks.

It is advisable to travel light as overhead luggage racks are only for lightweight, hand-held luggage and porters are not always available at stations. Coin lockers are often not large enough to accommodate your suitcases and staffed luggage rooms are found only at large stations.

Get the railway timetable from the Japanese National Tourist Organisation. To obtain your rail pass, buy an exchange order or voucher at any authorised agent before arrival. You exchange this for your JR Pass at any JR travel service office. Do not forget your passport.

It is advisable to reserve your seat. Reservations are made gratis at any JR travel service centre or at any *mirori-no-madoguchi* (green window) in a JR station. There are two passes available—ordinary and green, the latter entitling the holder to a seat in the first-class, spacious green cars. Seven-day passes are $270 (ordinary), $370 (green); 14-day passes are $430 (ordinary), $600 (green); and 21-day passes are $550 (ordinary), and $780 (green).

For further information and advice on where to purchase your JR voucher, contact the Japanese National Tourist Organisation.

12

Why bother flying business class?

O let us love our occupations,
Bless the squire and his relations,
Live upon our daily rations,
And always know our proper stations.

Charles Dickens, *The Chimes*

There seem to be some misconceptions regarding business-class travel on airlines. Business class (called different names by different airlines) is not restricted to briefcase-carrying, calculator-toting, downright, outright, forthright business executives. It is intended for anyone who would normally be paying full economy air fare. Almost anyone can travel in business class if they pay the fare. (I say almost, because some airlines do restrict the use of business class by children.)

The idea behind business class, a name chosen to assuage the fears of company accountants, is that passengers paying the full economy fare or the full economy fare plus a small supplement, are entitled to better treatment than the lumpen proletariat at the back of the aircraft. To me this seems fair enough. Passengers in business class tend to be frequent travellers similar to myself who need a little more comfort than the people in the back who are off on their annual holiday.

You probably gather I am a little uncertain of the morality of all this and I am ever willing to listen to a good argument for classless travel. Business class exists. I use it a lot because I work inflight and, when I get off the aircraft, I will probably be working within the hour. I need the extra space and comfort. That is my rationale and I am sticking with it.

What does the business-class traveller get for the extra money?

Flexibility of travel arrangements. Normally, if you are travelling on a standard business-class ticket, you can change dates of flight and, normally, carriers, without any hassle. This is not true of economy tickets sold under special conditions.

You get there. If the aircraft is full, which happens more and more these days, you have a better chance of getting a seat. If the worst comes to the worst, you can accept a downgrade to economy. But at least you will still get there.

A full-fare business-class ticket beats any discounted economy ticket in seat priority, any day.

You get more space. On all airlines, the seating in business class is far more spacious than in economy. (If you are a lumbering, overweight Welsh journalist, this is important.)

The seats are more comfortable. This depends to a certain extent on the airline, with one or two still naughtily using economy seats in business class. But most airlines have superior seats in business class.

You have special check-in facilities. You are invited, with

some airlines in some airports, into a special lounge to await your flight.

Your baggage is given priority.

How does all this work out in practice?

To find out, I flew British Airways BA10 from Sydney to Bangkok. It is widely accepted in the airline industry that British Airways is the game to beat in business class—BA's Club World is the envy of the other operators, all of whom have been forced to lift their game as a result.

There was a special check-in counter, which meant there were no queues. Fellow journalist Bill Mellor and I were invited into the British Airways lounge before take-off. Free drinks, canapés and a splendid cheese board.

When we boarded, we had aisle and window seats. In the cabin of this 747, the configuration was seven seats across. That is, two seats, an aisle, three seats, an aisle, then two seats. On a 747, that amounts to loads of space.

The seats we sat and slept in were the equivalent of first-class seats. They reclined and had foot props that rose automatically. As a connoisseur of business-class seats, where I seem to spend a major part of my life, I would say without hesitation that these are the most comfortable I have ever experienced. I see in a magazine that Cathay Pacific, in its advertising, is claiming to have 'the best seats in the world'. As I understand it, the new Cathay Pacific seats are made by the manufacturer who makes these armchairs for British Airways. Therefore, the advertising is probably right. These are the best seats in the world.

When we were safely strapped in, we were offered complimentary drinks, nuts and stereo head-sets (not the brain crunchers with tubes that you get in economy class). The plastic jars that the nuts come in are elegant and useful and I have a collection I now use for holding computer spare parts. The toiletry kit is a joy and everything in it follows design standards. The upholstery and the carpeting in the cabin exude style. All good gear.

The food was pretty standard for business class, which is very acceptable, and I guess was produced by Ansett in its flight-catering facility at Kingsford Smith. The wines were excellent, being a judicious mixture of Australian and French. I like an airline that serves Australian wines. It shows taste and style. The crew in the business-class area appear to have been imbued with a new spirit. Gone is the Roedean and Cheltenham Ladies' College condescension. (I once had a BA hostess come up to me when I was computing frantically away and say, 'Toys away, now. Time for tea'.)

The cabin staff appeared all to have come from the north of England and had a tremendous team spirit. Plainly, they liked working for British Airways. Plainly they revelled in the idea of serving in business class. And several of them were interested in my Compaq SLT computer, which shows an appreciation for the finer things in life.

Bill Mellor and I arrived in Bangkok refreshed, well fed and watered. The flight had gone quickly and pleasantly because of the intelligent attention of a most professional crew. That is what business-class travel is about and why I use it when I travel. Not because I am in business, but because I need my creature comforts.

First class—Is it worth it?

This is first class on British Airways. I am drinking a Château Talbot which is a 1982 and a Grand Cru Classe and is a bit better than your flagon red, I can tell you. The reason I am sitting here sipping this glorious drop from a glass which looks as if it were designed for one of the more intelligent members of the British aristocracy, is because I have been upgraded. That is, although my ticket reads business class, I have ended at the pointy end of the aircraft.

I am not one to let the side down, therefore I am wearing the Dunhill blazer, likewise the elegant necktie and the almost genuine Turnbull and Asser shirt. The outer raiment jarreth not. This is being written, but of course, on a computer. A first-class computer. The Atari Portfolio fits on my tray table between the aforementioned glass of the best that France can offer and an interesting vegetarian terrine which I'm investigating as a born again foodie. (Normally when I fly I list myself as a vegetarian because the food is, in my view, consistently better. But for first class I resume my normal earth bound, occasional meat-eating status.)

This is the new British Airways first class and someone has gone to a lot of trouble to see that this goes with this goes with that. At the back of my mind I vaguely recall the story that BA actually asked the passengers what they wanted. Such revolutionary behaviour appears to have paid dividends.

Everywhere one sees elegant small touches that make in-flight life more pleasant. The tray table swivels. This means I can attend a call of nature—something that comes with ever-increasing regularity as I get older—without having to ask someone to hold my tray. I can, indeed, extricate myself with the minimum of fuss.

The only odd note is struck with what the airlines call the amenity kit. On Qantas you get a leather zip pouch which contains various unguents to make the face less ugly and better smelling. It is difficult to put it more precisely.

On British Airways in first class you get something that looks like a miniature Father Christmas pressie sack. This contains sockettes and a grey pair of cloth slippers. But where is the natty gent's grooming kit as supplied by Qantas of which my friend, Gussie Fink-Nottle so approves? So far no sign.

I accost the most excellent and benevolent boniface who is responsible for our welfare. He says, and I take him at his word for he is, withal, a decent chap, that more follows. More does follow in between the terrine and the next course. This odd timing because I persisted, not because it was planned.

First up comes a toiletry kit with substantial, and I truly mean substantial, bottles of eau de cologne, after shave and other odiferous liquids. This in a leather case similar to that offered by Qantas, but in an elegant grey leather. (One wonders whether the airlines realise how these cases end up? Mine have labels stuck on them which say 'RS-232 connectors', '24000 modem', 'Telephone breaking tool kit' and so on. My computer travelling kit is elegant beyond belief.) The chief steward shimmers up once more and presents me with a six sided grey plastic case which contains a razor and a foam dispenser. Plus, note this well for I have never seen this on another aircraft, a towel.

The meal progresses. I opt for the beef consommé—just a dash of sherry to cool it— followed by the lamb. All excellent stuff giving lie to the oft repeated canard that first-class food—in every sense of that term—cannot be created in a jet liner. Indeed, it can. On this BA10 out of Sydney the miracle has occurred.

The movie is *Batman* which I have seen so I press two buttons and my chair turns into a fair imitation of a bed. A neat touch is that the blanket, in an attractive tweedy check, is all wool and doesn't pick up static. Head down now for a few *zzzs*. When I wake up we will be approaching Bangkok with just enough time for a late breakfast before disembarking. I can put up with this.

This is the way a gentleman should travel. Would that I could afford it. Next time back to business class, that which British Airways calls Club World. Nearly but not quite as good as first class.

Know your codes

Airlines have their own systems, their own peculiar language. The more you understand those systems, that language, the better.

For example, when your baggage is being ticketed make sure that the three code letters on the ticket represent the correct destination. Not once, but several times, we have caught inattentive counter clerks putting the wrong destination tags on baggage. Most of the codes are easy to remember: SYD is Sydney, MEL is Melbourne and so on. But there are some exceptions. HON is not Honolulu, it is Honduras. Honolulu is HNL. These codes are not only used on baggage destination tags, they are also used on the video sign boards at many airports.

Singapore is quite misleadingly labelled SIN. And Kota Kinabalu is BKI which is enough to confuse anyone.

London has two airports, London Heathrow—code LHR—and London Gatwick—code LGW. It is always worth checking which one you are using. A famous knighted Hong Kong magnate was flying from London to Hong Kong. He was delivered by his London staff to Heathrow although he was booked on Cathay Pacific and they leave from Gatwick. A helicopter was arranged to shuttle him between airports. He arrived at Gatwick airport just too late. His helicopter arrived as the Cathay Pacific flight took off.

Your airline also has a two letter code which shows on the ticket. Most are simple to follow. CX is Cathay Pacific, QF is Qantas and so on. Again, there are exceptions. Air New Zealand is TE because the airline used to be called TEAL.

When the airlines refer to you they normally use the word

PAX which has nothing at all to do with *Pax Romana* but is an abbreviation of passenger. Better still is VIP, initials which everyone understands. But so is CIP, this stands for Commercially Important Person.

On certain airlines on long routes you are passed out packages which contain toilet articles in meagre but usable quantities. These are splendidly called RON kits. It took diligent enquiry but we eventually found out that RON means Rest Over Night.

13

Reading an airline ticket

For mine own part, it was Greek to me.
William Shakespeare, *Julius Caesar, I,2*

Oh! rather give me commentators plain,
Who with no deep researches vex the brain;
Who from the dark and doubtful love to run,
And hold their glimmering tapers to the sun.
George Crabbe, *The Parish Register*

Winston Churchill said Russia was a 'riddle wrapped in a mystery inside an enigma'. He had not seen a modern airline ticket. Understanding what all of the cryptic messages and acronyms mean, what they stand for and what they indicate, makes solving the Rosetta stone a quick crossword, and breaking the Spektor code a kiddie's anagram.

The diagram on page 94 tells you what means what on most international air tickets and follows as closely as possible the rules, as laid down in IATA Ticketing Handbook, 1 April 88. The information, the book and the understanding of what it is all about was supplied to me by Travel Scene, the travel packagers in Edgecliff, NSW. The man who helped me was Bill Hollow, a friend for more than 30 years and an expert who has spent most of his life in the travel industry. But even he, experienced though he is, had to yell for assistance when he was giving me the good

oil on air tickets. In this chapter you see a very basic guide. The IATA guide—issued by the association to which most, but not all, airlines belong—takes 164 pages to give a simplified explanation.

We have left out the code for 'Minimum fare higher than banker's selling rate', the issuance of MCOs, miscellaneous charges orders; ERQ, request for endorsement; VUSA, visit USA fares, and other exotica.

The way in which a ticket can be read and interpreted, especially where it is complex, involving several carriers and several destinations, will vary according to who is doing the reading. Since the advent of computers and computerised tickets, the reading and writing of tickets has become much more standardised, but there is still room for leeway in interpretation.

This can work to your advantage. Just because the travel agent in Garra (there is no travel agent in Garra and, therefore, no one can be insulted) thinks that you cannot stop off in Hong Kong on the way to London does not mean that the airline involved agrees, or that someone at the airport may not read it slightly differently. This is because the number of permutations on a single ticket is, in effect, infinite.

If you travel to Europe with three stops each way the number of possible variations is something over ten million. This is why trying to work out your own itinerary without the assistance of an experienced and savvy travel agent is an exercise in futility.

HOW TO READ AND UNDERSTAND YOUR AIRLINE TICKET

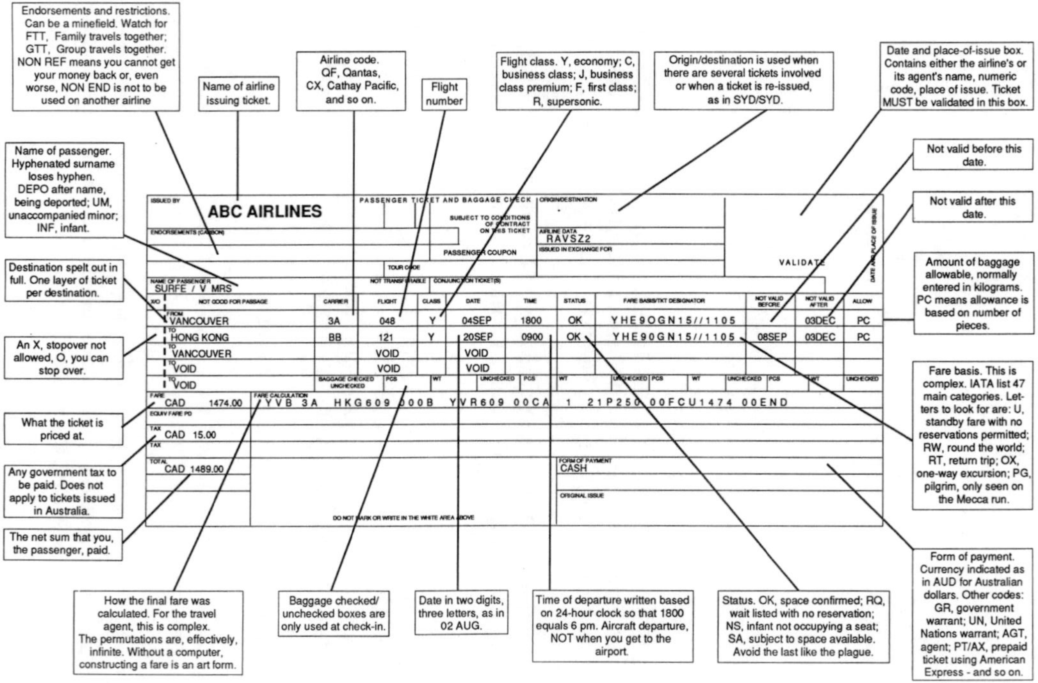

Some rules which agents and airlines break at their extreme peril include changing or leaving out the name of the passenger; changing the entry under 'Form of Payment'; making different entries on the top copy and the carbon copy of the same ticket. If anyone performs any of these deviations, then you are dealing with a shonky ticket.

Note that the staff at Travel Scene simply refused to allow a blank ticket to leave the premises, even for one hour to be photographed. IATA regulations are that tough and all bona fide agents adhere to them. These are some important points to check.

If you buy a ticket at an exceptionally cheap rate, check that it will actually let you get to your destination in the way that you intend and on the airlines you wish to travel on. If a change in your travel plans is possible, check that you can have the ticket rewritten and validated to another airline.

If you are travelling overseas, as soon as you get your ticket, take two photocopies. At the top of each photocopy write the name and address of the travel agent where you bought it and the name and address of the ticket issuer if it is different. Stick one photocopy to the lining inside your suitcase and give the other photocopy to someone you trust at home. If, heaven forbid, you should lose your ticket, this information will get you a new one re-issued in double quick time.

When you get to the first stop on your travels, reconfirm your ticket as soon as you get into your hotel. Many airlines do not insist on this confirmation, Qantas being a shining local example, but reconfirmation never does any harm.

If your ticket has codes you do not understand, ask for them to be explained. You should never end up with a ticket marked SUBLO, NON REV, NON END, but if you do, take my word for it, you are going to become very expert on the architecture of the world's airports. SUBLO means 'subject to load' which, in turn, means that everyone, but everyone, gets on before you do. The desperate people you see hanging around airports are not brigands, nor yet outcasts. They are passengers on SUBLO tickets who have been trying to get on an aircraft for some days. This is the legion of the damned and to be shunned.

14

The traveller's bookshelf

The books one reads in childhood, and perhaps most of all the bad and good bad books, create in one's mind a sort of false map of the world, a series of fabulous countries into which one can retreat at odd moments throughout the rest of life, and which in some cases can even survive a visit to the real countries which they are supposed to represent.

George Orwell, *Riding Down From Bangor*

Who that is busy to measure and compare
The heaven and earth and all the world large,
Describing the climates and folk of every place;
He is a fool and hath a grievous charge,
Without advantage . . .

Alexander Barclay, *The Ship of Fools, 1509*

The only way to get full value for your dollar when you travel is to read up on the places you are to visit, before you go. In Australia, we are singularly lucky in that we have based here the world's best guide-book publishing company, Lonely Planet Publications in Melbourne. The guides published by this company (which normally have the sub-title *A Travel Survival Kit*) are written with budget travellers in mind. This matters not. The information they contain applies to everyone.

There are now more than 24 titles on the list. All of them are

the best of their kind. Some of them are co-authored by Tony Wheeler, who also runs the company with his partner, Maureen. I have never clearly understood why these two have not been awarded the Order of Australia.

Another series of books which, like the Lonely Planet, cater for the traveller on a budget are published by Harvard Student Agencies and are called *Let's Go*. Ignore the quite awful title. The quality of the information provided is excellent. For example, in *Let's Go—France* the guide to restaurants in Paris worth eating at that you can actually afford is probably the best available. The writers and researchers for the books in this series are all students and they accept no free accommodation, no subsidised meals.

I checked its entry on Wales in *Let's Go—Britain* most carefully and it was accurate and illuminating. As is standard in these guides, it covered transportation first and then the history of the country followed by literature, food, language and then detailed accounts of each area. It can be forgiven for ignoring Caerwys, the town where I was born. It is not a major tourist destination. This book neatly handles the horrors of Welsh cooking by saying, 'Welsh cuisine is essentially the simple fare of a working nation'. Quite so.

Sadly, there is not a Lonely Planet or a Let's Go publication for everywhere in the world, so you will, therefore, have to make do with lesser publications such as the Michelin Guides. Wherever possible, I try to get the Michelin Green Guide to any city I visit. They are sometimes available only in French, but I still buy them and struggle through, dictionary in hand. For example, the only guide to Strasbourg worth considering is the Michelin Green, but there is no English edition.

These Michelin Green Guides are comprehensive, cultured and reasonably priced. There are also Michelin Red Guides, but I find them overwhelming in their detail and heavy to carry. The green ones fit in your pocket nicely. As I write this I have in front of me the *Michelin Green—Provence* and *Michelin Green—London*. The first in French, the second in English. The books are packed with the most detailed and splendidly drawn maps—in full colour. In the London book for example you do not just get maps of the various areas of London. You get detailed maps of the insides of museums. They both also have excellent introductions to the architecture of the area and this is most helpful when you are strolling around getting the feel of the place. These guides, incidentally, are still produced by the Michelin tyre company. The fat Michelin man made of tyres was originally designed in 1908.

I have also consistently found the Berlitz Travel Guides excellent value for money. They are small—sort of half paper-back size—typically 128 pages in length, very tightly written and accurate. Like all travel books, they eventually get out of date, but they appear to be regularly revised.

The APA Travel Guides were magnificent when first published, but seem to have fallen off of late. The very first, which was produced by Hans Hoefer and Star Black, was *Bali*. It was underwritten by the Inter-Continental Hotel management in Bali, a most praiseworthy deed. Hans took the pictures and designed the book, Star wrote the words. This was, at the time, probably the best illustrated travel book of its kind ever published. The pictures sang, the writing was competent, the quality of the printing was impeccable, the binding was lousy. Later titles have been of a lesser quality. Most are now sadly in need of updating. A recent book in this series on Dublin was almost a text book example of how not to write a travel guide. Over written, pretentious, boring. Beautiful pictures, lousy binding.

For consistent quality the Fodor Guides are hard to beat. They are constantly updated and the essays at the front of the book give the flavour of the country or city covered. On a recent trip to Florida with my family I used only the Fodor guide and we had a wonderful time. All the places recommended were exactly as described and all the advice worthwhile.

The best travel book writer in the world as far as I am concerned is the late H. V. Morton. The initials stand for Henry Vollam. I knew him quite well and he was a most erudite and pleasant cove. His books, which are still in print, are meticulously researched, elegantly written and full of fascinating detail.

Anyone visiting Italy, for example, must read *A Traveller in Italy* and, if possible, *A Traveller in Rome* as well. H. V. Morton died in 1979 but his books never date. He manages with his writing to get into the fabric of a place. To show the reader the warp and weft. A most marvellous writer. And a lovely man.

In the same style of writing, but not quite at the same superb and sustained level are the Blue Guides which are published by A. and C. Black. Although I know Britain well, having been born there, I keep *Blue Guide—Literary Britain* with me when I travel because it lets me know who wrote what where. And does it in a literate and intelligent style. This particular book is written by Ian Ousby who also wrote the *Blue Guide to England*, but all of the authors in the series are more than competent. The books in this series have a sure command of history, art and architecture. They all also have a strong point of view. Opinions are stated clearly and strongly. This I like.

In Asia there is a good series of books on the way of life in various countries called *Culture Shock*. These are published by Times Books out of Singapore and while not strictly guide-books in the full sense of the word they give an immediate feel for a place. They also show how to behave in public and carefully explain the taboos. I often wish that they were compulsory reading for all tourists.

I have a great fondness for guide-books which show the undiscovered and unusual aspects of a place. Such a book is *Weird and Wonderful America* by Laura A. Bergheim. If I am travelling to the United States it tells me the site of the Black Madonna and where I can see the world's largest Holstein Cow and where to find a roadside sign which says, 'Lady, if he won't stop, hit him on the head with a shoe'. And many other jollities.

My kind of information. Useless and entertaining. Perfect loo-side reading.

Before I go to any new country I try to learn a smattering of the language—even if it is only to say 'good morning' and 'thank you'. This is, I think, a politeness and appreciated almost everywhere you go, with the possible exception of Hong Kong. There you can either speak Cantonese with all seven tones or you cannot. There is no middle ground.

Australia is well served with guide-books. The best all round guides in my view are the travel books published by Reader's Digest. I am not a lover of the magazine itself, but these books are truly magnificent.

My partner got *The Coast of New South Wales* for Christmas and we fight over it. It has the most amazing aerial shots I have ever seen and I have no idea how they were taken. They make the best pictorial guides to an area you could possibly imagine. Recently, in the stunning new National Parks and Wildlife Service centre at Audley, I bought a sister volume, *National Parks of New South Wales*. It is pretty nearly as good, but lacks those amazing aerial photographs and uses scenic shots instead. There are books covering all of the other states and they are all of this very high standard.

Finally free travel guides. Almost every nation on earth welcomes tourists and produces brochures and pamphlets and guides to make a visit more pleasurable. You have to approach these guides with considerable care because they are not written to show you the negative aspects of a place. Providing you keep in mind that the writer is wearing a pair of rose coloured spectacles and the publisher, the government or tourist agency concerned, has an axe to grind, they are well worth collecting.

15

Cruising

As idle as a painted ship
Upon a painted ocean.
Samuel Taylor Coleridge, *The Rime of the Ancient Mariner*

Only fools and passengers drink at sea.
Alan John Villiers, *Australia naval commander*

Cruise ships and cruising did not enter my life until fairly late on. My only early experience was on troop ships and this is not the same thing at all. My first cruise was just over a month ago and I can report dispassionately on the advantages (many) and the disadvantages (few) of cruising.

The first great advantage is that you meet fascinating people. A cruise ship attracts all sorts and conditions of people. There are, for example, cruising fanatics who cruise, almost literally, from one year's end to the next. Whose real home is an outside cabin on a cruise ship. One couple on board the *Ocean Pearl*, the first cruise ship that I have travelled on, were on their 37th cruise. This is not thought unusual by the other passengers.

One morning, at breakfast, the other five people at my table nonchalantly swapped stories about cruising in Alaska—one couple had been three times, one couple once—drifting through the Caribbean and cruising the Baltic. For them, it is a way of life. Since taking the cruise—is that the right verb?—I have been

doing some investigation and come up with some amazing figures.

Most cruises, especially from Australia, sell out top down. That is, the most expensive cabins go first, the cheapest cabins go last. There are perpetual cruisers—is that the right term?—who make cruise ships their floating homes. There is one lady in Australia who has her own double bed hoisted aboard.

Many passengers on cruise ships do not get off at ports of call. At first I did not believe this but personal experience now convinces me it is so. There is a percentage of passengers who get on a cruise ship and stay there. They have been abroad, thank you very much, and they will stay precisely where they are, where everyone speaks English, the water is safe and there is no danger from disease and sun stroke.

The people on my first cruise liner, the *Ocean Pearl*, were divided like ancient Gaul into three parts. (My understanding is that this applies to almost all cruise ships at the top end of the market.) The three parts are the old and rich; the young and cruise crazy; the ship's staff. All these groups are interesting to talk to, to mix with.

There seems to be a mistaken idea that because people are old and rich they are, by definition, therefore dumb and boring. Nothing could be further from the truth. Age has never equalled mental infirmity. Riches, equally, rarely equate with total stupidity.

On this short cruise I have had more intelligent conversations then I would have in six months in Sydney. These people have lived; have had experiences well worth the recounting; no longer worry about the world's esteem. As a result they are interesting and informative. They give the lie to the glib clichés that say that cruising is for the newly wed and the nearly dead.

With age comes eccentricity. I am a collector of eccentricities. Sadly, it was the cruise before this one that was graced by one of the inheritors of the Hearst newspaper fortune. She, I am reliably informed, had her limousine airfreighted to every port that the *Ocean Pearl* called at so that she could take in the sights in style.

On this voyage, on board this ship the *Ocean Pearl*, is a voyager who is also an ardent amateur musician. He is a bassoonist. The bassoon is a solitary instrument. Not an instrument that lends itself to socialising. There is, indeed, not much music written for solo bassoon playing. Merely parts in various scores. The bassoon is as lonely and as lowly as Tubby the Tuba. This enthusiastic bassoon player from Sydney has brought his bassoon with him. In his cabin, from time to time, he practises. He is not, in truth, a professional player although he plays with two amateur orchestras in Sydney. He says that he failed in his audition with the Willoughby Symphony Orchestra.

I discussed this with another passenger as we waited in a rain storm on the island of Sumatra. He thought bringing a bassoon on a cruise was not quite the article. He himself played the French horn. He had brought only the mouthpiece for the purposes of practise.

The first delight of cruising, then, is the people you meet.

The next delight is the food. On *Ocean Pearl* we were fed to bursting point. Coffee and biscuits or tea and small cakes (what used to be called tea and tabnabs) were available from 6 o'clock in the morning. Then came breakfast which was a multi-course affair served in two different dining rooms. For those who felt a little peckish at 11 o'clock there was further coffee and tea with assorted nibbles.

Lunch was always a major affair with several courses and accompanying wines. Tea time, let us not forget tea time, came at four and, once again, coffee and tea and biscuits and cakes were brought to the starving masses.

Bit of a tricky lapse there between tea and the second sitting of dinner which was at eight o'clock. To keep us sedated we were offered cocktail snacks with our, indeed, cocktails. Dinner was five courses, again with wine and liqueurs. After which one repaired to the bar or the disco—depending on age and inclination—to try and settle some of it down before sleeping.

If, in the middle of the night, starvation struck, a press on the steward's call button brought sandwiches, munchies, hamburgers, what have you, at the fast trot. Never in my life have I eaten so well and so often. Hog heaven.

The second delight of cruising is controlled environment. On this trip we went on a ride into the hills of the Sumatran island of Nias where we saw the amazing wall jumpers of Watamabatlao. We rode up to the village in trucks fitted with planks as seats. On our way back we were drenched to the skin by a thunderstorm. Hard lying conditions, especially for those not used to it. When we returned to the ship there was a large sign hung over the side. It said, 'Welcome Home'. The crew lined the gangway and clapped us aboard. We had returned to the womb.

With welcoming comforts such as this, one can rough it for a few hours with equanimity.

The third delight is the impossibility of ever being bored. There is something happening each minute of the day, although there is no pressure for you to take part. Starting with gentle warm-up exercises first thing in the morning to shuffleboard during the day to variety shows in the evening to disco until the small hours, each minute has some form of entertainment on offer. Every member of the crew was dedicated to keeping the passengers entertained, fed, watered and happy for every second of the voyage.

A case in point. We passed Krakatoa and the captain made a special effort to see that we did this in the afternoon so that we could see it first in perfect clarity and then changing colour as the sun sank. While this was going on the first officer gave a commentary on when the volcano erupted, the results, the aftermath. He was as informed as any university lecturer—and three times as entertaining.

The standard of entertainment was very high. On the last night I watched four stunning young ladies in rubberised, black mini dresses do a high kicking routine to a jazzed up version of Three Little Maids from School. Considering the average age of the males in the audience I thought this a little risky. Certainly my heart was beating at an unaccustomed rate.

What then are the disadvantages? Perhaps because of my upbringing I am opposed to tipping. On cruise ships it is mandatory and when you budget for a trip you must add ten per cent to the total cost for tipping. Sad but essential. That is the only disadvantage that I noticed.

Will I go again?

Sure. This is back to the womb time, folks. No cares, no thought for the morrow, no decision to make larger than whether to have the duckling or the salmon for dinner. If a holiday, by definition is a change of pace, a relief from, everyday concerns—then cruising is, by that definition, the perfect holiday.

Advice

When going on a cruise for the first time, cast from your mind any ideas of tall, handsome gigolos in white dinner jackets offering cocktails to elegant young things wearing gownless evening straps. Forget any ideas you may have obtained from watching *Doctor at Sea*, where Brigitte Bardot bares her all for Dirk Bogarde.

Cruises are not like that any more. Modern cruises are about travel with the minimum of fuss. When you cruise, you become similar to a maritime snail. You take your home—your supremely comfortable home—with you, as you visit some of the exotic outposts of the world.

To enjoy cruising, you need to be in a specific mind set before you go. Cruises are not designed, are not totally suitable, for people who do not like the human race, who do not like its dirty face. Cruises are not for the recluse, the unsociable. Cruises are, in the main and on the main, highly structured floating hotels. They are organised. Not in a pushy assertive way, but organised nevertheless. With everything from meal times to fancy-dress parties run under control and on time.

On board, there are more facilities than you would ever get, even in the most luxurious land-locked hotel. And there will be organised activities such as cookery classes, history lectures, keep-fit aerobics. There will be a ship's newspaper to keep you vaguely in touch with what is happening in the land-locked world. This is of no moment to you. You are secure and serene in your floating time warp.

To truly enjoy a cruise, you must allow yourself to be catered for, to be cosseted, to be comforted. Try anything else and you will rock the boat.

Some practical tips

Before you book, check that you will have enough room. Ascertain the tonnage of the ship (cruises are shamelessly pre-metric) and divide by the number of passengers. If there are more than 40 tons a passenger, all is well. Between 25 and 30, you will start to feel a little restricted. If the figure is below 20, it means you will be cramped for space. Fine for a short trip between ports. Not acceptable for long cruises.

Check the steward–to–passenger ratio (using the word in a unisex way). On a luxury cruise, it is one steward to three passengers: 1 to 10 is not uncommon and not unpleasant on shorter cruises. Anything below that is poor. My simple check is this. Do they serve breakfast in bed in your cabin on request? (The fact that I never have breakfast in bed has nothing to do with the validity of this question.)

Do not worry over much about seasickness. Most modern cruise ships have stabilisers and anti-seasickness remedies get cheaper by the day. I am the proud holder of the record of having been seasick in the Suez Canal. Modern medication can calm even my queasy stomach. You, being made of finer and nobler stuff, will have no troubles at all.

Take the same amount of luggage as you would on an air trip. True, there is no weight allowance on a cruise ship. And, true, the social activities invite dressing up. But a cabin trunk in your cabin gets in the way and most of the gear inside never gets used. One suitcase is enough.

(That most readers will totally ignore this advice goes without saying.)

Costs. There is a general impression that cruising is expensive, a hobby only for the filthy rich. This is just not so. In many cases, it is indeed a bargain holiday. To work out how much a cruise really costs you, it is essential that you compare like with like. With a cruise ship, you get all your meals and all your accommodation and all your travel expenses paid in the one hit. You will be staying in the equivalent of a three-, four- or five-star hotel and you will be taking every meal at an expensive restaurant. Your only extra expenses will be drink and tips. And the drink will be cheaper than most places ashore. Costed this way cruises are the way to live the life of a maritime Riley.

Book early. Out of Australia, and, indeed, most other places in the world, cruises tend to fill up very quickly. The best berths, the most desirable cabins, are often snapped up as soon as the cruise is announced. Horace, in his first Epistle, records: 'We work hard at doing nothing: we look for happiness in boats...' Sounds better in the original Latin, but it describes modern cruising perfectly: doing nothing and looking for—and finding—happiness.

16

Driving yourself

If I had no duties, and no reference to futurity, I would spend my life in driving briskly in a post-chaise with a pretty woman.
Samuel Johnson, *Life of Johnson by James Boswell*

The car has become the carapace, the protective and aggressive shell, of urban and suburban man.
Marshall McLuhan, *Understanding Media.*

The driving is like the driving of Jehu, the son of Nimshi; for he driveth furiously.
2 Kings, ix, 20

You may recall that when you passed the driving test the strongest feeling was that of total independence. You could go anywhere (within reason) and do anything (also within reason) without having to wait on the availability and willingness of someone else. A most glorious feeling. And that is what you mostly get when you hire a car on holidays and business trips. Independence. The ability to go pretty much anywhere, any time, as it pretty much pleases you.

You can book a car before you travel—through your travel agent or a car-hire company—get a car when you arrive at an airport, or get a car once you have settled in. All these methods have their pluses and minuses.

Before you travel

Providing the booking is confirmed and reconfirmed, there is a good chance that you will get what you want and that it will be ready for you when you arrive.

Advantages. This semi-certainty of delivery (and fixing any problems when you arrive is normally very simple) is a weight off the mind. Sometimes you may get a better price if there is a special promotion operating. This is especially true of fly/drive holidays. If the car-hire company has stuffed up—not a totally unknown event—and let out all the cars in the class you have booked, you should be upgraded at no extra charge.

Disadvantages. You can lose special discounts that you might be able to arrange. Also, if your travel plans change rapidly, you may well spend more time and money rearranging and reorganising than you would otherwise save.

Finally, if you have to return the car to the airport at the end of your stay, you will need to add at least an hour to your departure time because at most airports the procedure of returning hire cars is as fast as a thousand rushing tortoises.

Airport

Advantages. This leaves your schedule open and you are not stuck with specific dates and times. Another advantage is that you may well be able to negotiate a very favourable price. My belief is that, if you have the front of a Mack truck, you can get the quoted price down considerably. I have just tested this at London Heathrow airport. When the price was quoted at a major car-hire counter, I said firmly that I was a member of the Icelandic Herring Fisheries Commission and was, therefore, entitled to the standard discount (I had no idea what a standard discount might be). I got ten per cent off, without showing a single scrap of paper.

Disadvantages. The great disadvantage is that in the high season there may not be the class of car that you require. The cheapest cars always seem to go first. The monster disadvantage is that there may be no cars at all.

Again, if you have to return the car to the airport, you need to add an extra hour for departure.

Hotel

This may cost more—the cost of transport to and from the airport—but the hassle it saves often makes it well worthwhile. Anyone who has arrived at Charles de Gaulle airport on a rainy Friday afternoon and then tried to drive into the centre of Paris has had a true foretaste of hell. Your hotel may well be able to recommend a local dealer who can provide a car at a substantially lower price than the big car-hire companies, although then you need to check the quality of the car with some care.

When you hire a car you are given a form full of small print which you are asked, nay instructed, to sign on the spot. I have taken legal advice on this and the general opinion appears to be that much, if not most, of the contract is unenforceable because:

- The clauses are in typeface—5 point Gibberish or 6 point Myopia—that is something less than easily legible.
- The implications of the clauses are not verbally explained.
- Pressure is applied to make you sign the form on the spot and not give careful consideration to its contents.

None of this matters very much with the major companies, providing you take full collision insurance. While it is true the companies almost certainly make a profit on this extra insurance, the peace of mind in knowing that you are fully covered outweighs the extra cost.

If you do not take out that extra insurance, the idea is that you are totally responsible for the car and you must make quite sure that all defects—especially in the bodywork—are listed on the form and accepted by the renter. This, in theory, can be done. In practice, all you want to do is to get away. Best bet is always to take the extra insurance.

General tips

• Only hire cars with automatic gearboxes. It makes life much easier.
• Take an internationally accepted credit card. In theory you can use cash to rent a car, but it is very difficult. In the US it appears to be impossible to hire without a credit card and it is extremely difficult in most other countries.
• You must have your licence. In most cases a standard Australian licence—provided it is current—will do, but in a few countries an international licence is needed.
• If you have a companion who is going to drive, make sure both names are listed on the hire form, otherwise the insurance cover will not be valid.
• In some countries never hire a self drive car. The reasons vary.

Sometimes because the traffic is so tough within the city and parking impossible, for example Rome, Brussels and, marginally, Paris. (This is not to say you should not hire a car for travelling from those cities and touring the surrounding countryside. The problem area is in the city itself.)

Sometimes the cost of a driver makes no difference to the cost of hiring a car—the Philippines, Indonesia, and, to some extent, Malaysia. In the Philippines it is frequently cheaper to hire a car with a driver than without.

Sometimes because in any accident you will always be to blame and may very well end up in jail—this problem exists to a greater or lesser extent in Turkey, much of the Gulf, especially Saudi Arabia, and parts of Africa. In these matters both your travel agency and your car-hire company will be able to advise you. Take their advice.

• Most cars hired out by the big organisations are rarely more than a year old. And, in theory, they are serviced and given the valet treatment between each hiring, although I have found things on the back seat which I would not like to discuss. Before you drive off, find out whom you call if the car should break down. Breakdowns do happen. A major hirer rented me a car to drive from London airport to Thornton Heath, a distance of about 40 km. It took three changes of car to get me there .

• If you have trouble with the constabulary in a foreign country, smile and speak slow English and offer every document you can lay your hands on. Never offer a bribe unless you know precisely what you are doing. A surprising number of police officers around the world take a very narrow view of attempts to bribe and corrupt. Pleasant, slightly anxious co-operation is the ticket.

• Never drive when you are tired. It is difficult enough in all conscience to adjust to a new car, a new landscape, strange signs and foreign names without adding this extra burden.

• Get the car company to provide you with any maps that are available. I carry strips of transparency—cut from an overhead-projector transparency sheet—and write on it with marker pen the various identifying points and turns on a route that I have sorted out from road maps. I then stick the strip to the side of the windscreen with Magic Putty. As I am driving along I can check my route in a head-up position.

Europe

Oh, when I was young and easy I drove all over Europe. In style. I explored almost every European country from the Arctic Circle down to the Mediterranean in a series of vehicles that ranged from a Citroen 2CV to a Rolls Royce. It was this last car that I later tried to import to Australia, leading to embarrassing questions in the House. Assorted politicians thought it was cheeky for someone on an assisted passage to have a Roller in the hold. In the end I sold the Rolls and paid full fare.

I drove everywhere because my life, my loves, my travels were all unstructured. Travelling around in a car meant that I could take all my impedimenta with me. No need to worry about packing tidily. No need to worry about packing at all. Dump everything into the boot and on to the back seat and take off. Certain rules helped ease my way and I commend them to you.

Whenever possible stick to the by-roads.

Always stop driving by 4 pm unless you have booked a hotel room.

Never let the tank get lower than half full.

Invest heavily in maps.

Never, like Jehu son of Nimshi, play at boy racers.

Always carry a small tent as a fall-back position for *le camping*.

Never pick up a hitchhiker .

Using this system I toured Europe for both business and pleasure for several years. There were the odd moments, the occasional problem, the temporary hiccup. Now, through the mists of time, even the occasional breakdown seems a pleasurable experience.

To see if the Grand Tour of Europe by car is still feasible I have, over the past few months, been driving around Britain and Europe. In Margaret Thatcher's mind these are two distinctly different places.

In Britain I borrowed a Volvo 740 Turbo station wagon. I normally use Volvos of a milder breed, of slightly less verve than this model and at the lower end of the price scale. This car had everything in it including heated wing mirrors and seats. With it I drove from Sussex to Hereford and South Wales with my family ensconced inside. This station wagon (estate car is Volvo's preferred term) swallowed the luggage and still had large areas of storage space left over. The power of its engine allowed overtaking to be almost a reflex action and cruising at motorway speeds a silent pleasure. The seating kept me comfortable by the hour. Like all large Volvos, this vehicle is a gentle person's conveyance.

The first rule in driving in Britain is to avoid the motorways like the plague. They appear to be constantly under repair and often choked with traffic and traffic jams of Guinness Book of Records proportions. The worst I encountered was on the M25 which is a ring road around London. When first designed over a decade ago, it was seen as a permanent solution to London's traffic problems. I laugh lest I burst into tears.

Shun then, the motorways. Instead, use the A roads with the occasional excursion on to those designated B. My own feeling is that if you are driving for pleasure, not business, this advice applies throughout Europe. Autobahns, autostradas and routes national are all very well if you are in a hurry; a pain if you are out for enjoyment. Most of the minor roads have better surfaces than Australia's major highways, which is, admittedly, not saying much.

On this trip I drove through England and Wales down to the Gower, which is that little England beyond Wales. It was the height of a most amazing British summer; eye-achingly green trees, a smell of clover, old men with knotted handkerchiefs on their heads. We drove with the sun-roof wide open.

The second rule of driving in Britain (and in much of Europe) is to take your food with you and eat al fresco. It used to be that you could stop at a pub and eat a ploughman's lunch with half a pint of warm, wet bitter pulled from the wood. No more. The restaurants on the motorways induce anorexia nervosa in the traveller. Avoid them like the plague. When motoring in Britain, it is always better to take your lunch with you and sort out decent restaurants for dinner when you arrive. Anyway I find a heavy lunch soporific.

It is important that you drive with, as the legal phrase has it, due care and consideration. This is to save on the wear and tear on your nerves and the fuel bill. Petrol is ruinously expensive in Britain and even more expensive in other countries. Work on the basis that you are paying half as much again for gas as you would in Australia and, generally, you will not be far wrong.

There is a reciprocal arrangement between Australian motorist's associations, the NRMA, the RACV etc. and its equivalent in Britain, the AA. This is a free service. You apply to the NRMA at this end and then front up at any AA office in Britain. There you will be given a year's free membership and a copy of the AA Handbook which has most excellent maps of Britain.

United States

It is far easier to drive on the right-hand side of the road than you would imagine. Most of the the rest of the world does it already with no problem at all. Driving in America is, I promise you, much easier than driving up the Killer Hume or down the Bulli Pass to Wollongong.

In the United States the car is king. It has been since Henry Ford produced the Ford T in any colour you liked as long as it was black.

In America you can do anything in a car except, perhaps, be born. Children can be, and are, conceived in cars if only by accident. You can watch movies, or pretend to watch movies; you can bank; buy dog biscuits; deposit and collect your dry-cleaning; look upon the embalmed remains of a loved one; eat what many Americans foolishly believe is a gourmet meal. You can, indeed, live your life in a car. Many Americans do.

No one knows why the Americans drive on the opposite side of the road to us. All theories are farcical supposition. All that can be safely asserted is that it is so. For Americans the right side is the right side.

Driving on this side becomes perfectly natural after the first three or four kilometres. After that it only impinges on your consciousness when you have to decide which way to turn at a crossing. The right-hand driving position means that all the controls are on the wrong side. The answer is to never drive anything except a car with an automatic gearbox. Otherwise you, too, will find yourself winding down the window when you fondly believe you are changing gear from third to fourth.

There are some minor changes in nomenclature. The bonnet becomes the hood; the boot, a trunk; a small car, a sub-compact; and petrol, gas. Nothing to worry about.

The road systems are a little different. Mainly they are more efficient. The United States has freeways, turnpikes and back roads. Easy to understand. Freeways are free. On turnpikes you pay. Back roads are slower but more fun. Most road signs are much the same as they are here although there are some anomalies. The book—and later the movie—*Last Exit to Brooklyn* came from a road sign which you see as you drive in from Kennedy airport to Manhattan. 'Squeeze right' is understandable where three lanes become two. 'Yield' means Give Way. 'Ped Xing' means that there is a pedestrian crossing ahead. Navigation is no major problem. American road numbering is logical and relatively easy to follow.

Other points to notice:

Gas stations are very much less prevalent than they are in other countries. For example, you can drive from Tampa to

Miami on turnpikes and you will not pass a single gas station on the way. If your gauge shows less than half full, top up at the next gas station.

Unless you are in a hurry to get somewhere, the best bet is to avoid turnpikes and drive on the back roads. Turnpikes are boring and have a multitude of very bad advertising signs which are 30 metres high and invite you to retire to an adult community or eat in a fast food joint that specialises in instant heartburn. Driving on the back roads, which is more pleasant, is called shunpiking. All it requires is minimal map-reading skills.

In theory the speed limit is 55 miles an hour (about 88 kilometres an hour) except on some turnpikes where it goes as high as 65 miles an hour. In fact, the traffic seems to move at about 10 miles an hour faster on turnpikes and freeways. On any other roads speeding is a no-no as instant fines are issued to transgressors.

American police come in all varieties and shades. If you are pulled over stay in your car and have your licence ready. Make no sudden moves because if you do you may well find yourself staring down the muzzle of a Magnum .357. Fines are normally paid on the spot. Most police will accept travellers' cheques but not credit cards.

In most States you can filter right at a traffic light when it is red as if it were a 'give way' sign. On the other hand, U-turns are illegal almost everywhere.

Your Australian driving licence will be recognised but it is much safer to get an international driving licence from the NRMA.

Hiring a car—the Americans call it renting—is much cheaper in the United States than here. You must have a credit card. In most places you can hire cars at one location and leave them at another. Beware of being upgraded unless you positively, absolutely know it is free. It rarely is. Also make sure that you know precisely what you will be billed when you return the car. Many companies have vaguely defined extras which are only explained to you clearly at the end of a hiring.

Parking can be tricky and expensive in big cities. Never park by a fire hydrant which is normally short and squat and painted red. Never park in a towaway zone or you will, literally, be towed away.

In the north, especially the north-east, snow is commonplace in the winter and is a major hazard. Approach driving in snow the way a hedgehog makes love, with great care.

It is, quite correctly, absolutely illegal to pass a stationary school bus—large, old-fashioned and normally painted yellow—if its lights are flashing. This means children are getting on and off. Traffic in both directions must remain stationary until the school bus moves off. A splendid law.

Driving in America is easier on the nerves than driving in Australia. The roads are better; the standards of driving are much higher; the signposting is clearer. Yes, you will be driving in a foreign country and, yes, you will be driving on what you think is the wrong side of the road. But it truly is no great hassle. Try it. You'll like it.

Other motoring tips

An international driving licence is well worthwhile. True, in some countries you can drive on the Australian licence, but some of the gendarmerie out in the boondocks simply do not believe that one ill-typed piece of paper a licence makes. Get your international licence from your local motoring organisation. (You will need two passport photographs.) This is valid for one year.

You must have the registration papers if it is your own car. If it is a hire car the document to look for is a Hire Registration Certificate.

Do not try to break any records. Often, you will be driving on the other side of the road in strange territory. Cannon-ball runs are foolhardy, tiring and counter-productive. I refuse to drive more than 300 kilometres in any one day on my trips and I demand, and get, rest days between.

If you are hiring a car, consider a judicious mixture of train travel and locally hired cars to cut down the amount of driving.

Work on the basis that all other drivers are as mad as cut snakes. This is undoubtedly true in France and Italy and, to a lesser extent, in Belgium. Avoidance is the key word.

You must have full medical insurance before you travel. Medicare does not, repeat *not*, cover you for overseas travel although some countries have reciprocal agreements with Australia. Your travel agent will advise you but you need more insurance than you think.

On driving across Australia

The tradition of driving a motor car for sheer enjoyment—as an end to itself instead of a means of getting somewhere—is gradually disappearing. It is being eroded, diminished, circumscribed by speed limits, draconian penalties, traffic jams and unleaded petrol. The romance, sadly, is going out of our driving.

The idea of driving as a pleasure, as a means to an enjoyable end, reached its apogee in England during the early 1950s when petrol rationing was just ending and traffic jams had yet to make an appearance. The Poms took this pleasure—as they take all pleasures—seriously. Cars were, of course, kept sparkling clean. Washed, leathered, waxed, adorned like Solomon. Were they not the centre of existence? A trip in the country, no matter how short, was a matter not to be taken lightly.

Longer distances required sterner measures. A 300 kilometre drive meant the car would be specially overhauled, route maps prepared, luncheon and refreshment stops planned. D-Day revisited.

In Australia we do not take such matters seriously. We get in the car and then drive great distances—great by European standards—with barely a second thought. This is the way we drove to Perth.

Perth seems an ideal destination for a quick spin in the country. Navigation is simple—keep Australia on your left—and the roads are, relatively for Australia, in good condition. And very straight. Because of speed restrictions, flying policemen and instantaneous radar fixes it is probably impossible to drive the distance very quickly. I have it on good authority that it is theoretically possible to drive from Sydney to Perth in less than thirty hours. That it may, indeed, be possible to cram 3164 kilometres into 24 hours of driving. This is not allowable under the current laws. Therefore I have no idea whether such speedy long distance driving is possible. Although it does sound feasible.

The roads of Australia, while not to be compared with the autostrada of Italy and the autobahnen of Germany, have two great virtues. Outside of city limits and away from the dreaded Hume Highway they are relatively traffic free. And, except when traversing the few mountain ranges we have, they tend to run as straight as a die for kilometre after kilometre. There were two of us and we were driving a brand new sparkling Volvo 760 GLE. These days I almost invariably drive Volvos. They are the ultimate brisk carriages for gentlefolk. Roomy, quiet, air-conditioned, leather upholstery, excellent high fidelity on the radio and an overall feeling of almost Victorian stability and solidity. Totally sure-footed and secure at all times, yet able, when asked, to sprint like a boy racer. No vulgar ostentation. A lot of discreet style. Very much my sort of vehicle.

We left quite early one morning—a good time to start any journey of moment—and eased our way up through Parramatta to face the obstacle that Wentworth first conquered—the Blue Mountains. The road leads through Richmond and Windsor with its elegant white church that makes the Gothic revival almost worthwhile. Then up, up into the singing mountains flying over Bellbird Hill on Bell's Line of Road. Names of pure romance. Names for a Theroux to conjure with.

As you come down from these lovely heights we see the sign which welcomes you to greater Lithgow. Dear Lord, what then must lesser Lithgow be like? Then through what the New South Wales government in a misplaced attack of humour called the Orange growth area. And in doing so lost millions and millions of our money on a grandiose scheme that forgot to realise that where people want to live is more important than where town planners say they should.

We get to Molong and leave the traffic, the fumes, the people, the great wen of Sydney behind. We enter the wonder that is the country of Australia. Being Welsh I was brought up on country which was either slag or ferns, little in between, with a haze of blue mountains away over there in the rain. (In my youth it was always raining in Wales.) Australia is very different. Not, as people keep telling me, harsher, as if that was some form of vulgar complaint, but different. Red and ochre and brown and silver gum trees and tall grass—tall as a big kangaroo—and dams seen in the distance and farm buildings eye-hurting silver in the sun. Only in Australia has the use of corrugated iron to produce pleasing architectural shapes been brought to an art form.

Near Molong the fields are brown and gold because there is a distinct lack of rain. In other countries, other times, this would be a full blown drought. Not in this corner of Australia. Not yet. From Molong to Wellington and then on from there where we drive along roads which are arrow straight for ever. The longest stretch we measured, where you could see from one end to the other, was 27 kilometres long. A corner becomes a blessing to let you exercise the steering wheel.

Through Nyngan to Wilcannia. Here we saw for the first time a phenomenon which was to occur again and again on this minor epic journey. On these Great Western plains the land is flat to the horizon, so flat you can see the curvature of the earth. I had never seen this, not knowingly, but there it was. An argument that no member of the Flat Earth Society could refute. The world is indeed a globe and we are part of it.

From Wilcannia and passing Triple Chance (what story is hidden in that name?) to Broken Hill with its Trades Hall looking like the municipal buildings of Pontypridd but with sunshine and no soot. Solidly inappropriate Victorian architecture standing ill at ease in this true, frontier mining town. Leaving Broken Hill the scene changes subtly yet again. It is not a foreign country, just a different part of Australia. Drivers are more courteous, road signs are different. 'Lake View Hotel. Opp. Northern Mine'. One, pointing in the direction from which we have come says, 'Broken Hill–Sydney–Joh's Country'. Now it is no longer apposite.

By Broken Hill we have covered 1180 kilometres, just over a quarter of the journey. Downhill now, southwards, to Port Augusta. From Peterborough we are driving across the tag end of the Flinders Ranges and before reaching Port Augusta we come over Horrocks Pass which is picturesque and wonderfully full of curves and twists. Horrocks, the man who found it, died, quite young, in a shooting accident. Sad.

Down to Port Augusta which is salt flats, some white, some red (From hematite? Probably.) Then past Iron Knob, ugly and depressing with open cast mining, to Kimba which boasts it is halfway across Australia, having little or nothing else to boast about. But it is not halfway to Perth from Sydney. At Kimba we have covered 1755 kilometres. 2245 to go. From the next main town on this route, Ceduna, the road skirts rather than runs across the Nullarbor Plain. (My favourite trivia is that the Nullarbor is the only major landmark in Australia with a Latin name—*null arbor*, no trees). It has trees but not many. The wind blows hot and dry. Hotter and drier than I would believe.

The Volvo has a modern fitting called climate control. Set the wheel to the temperature we want and then forget it. At the beginning of the journey I set it to chilly English summer. And then forgot it. We stop on the Nullarbor and step out. It is 44 degrees in the shade and no shade. The wind is gusting 20 knots. And in our upholstered, steel cocoon we know not. Neither do we care.

Does this insulation from the rigours of the Australian climate make our travel less enjoyable, less worthwhile, less real? Are we missing out on the real Australia? I think not. The real Australia is now air-conditioned. Difficult to tell where the Nullarbor starts and where it ends but crossing it could be judged to be a thousand kilometre journey, give or take, by and large.

There are signs that we are skirting a great wasteland. The petrol stations offer salt water to wash down your windscreens, the remedy worse than the cure. All drivers make a mystic Masonic signal to each other as they pass. Hands remain on the steering wheel but the fingers of the left hand are extended straight up in salute. The message is, I'm going orright, mate. How about you? A comforting kinship. On the road mainly are thunderous trucks roaring full to Perth, empty back again. And convoys of caravans who believe because they move sedately in clusters they are not a hazard on the road. A dangerous complacency hard to puncture. And, unbelievably, a French couple on bicycles who intend to cycle across the Nullarbor, camping as they go.

Western Australia. Once across the border into Western Australia there are mobile road taxation collection stations with Police writ large over the side. In the middle of the Nullarbor where there is no other traffic to be seen in any direction, where the road is clear for 10 to 20 kilometres, they come towards us, raise their hands in greeting and then stop and fine us because we are driving at ten kilometres over the speed limit. One feels outrage, not remorse.

Leaving the Nullarbor is a subtle movement, a segue from one

Australia to another. Slowly the trees thicken, adopt more civilised shapes; small bushes dress the landscape. Soon it appears as if some mystic gardener, a reincarnated Australian Capability Brown, has created a natural park and then groomed it into civilised submission. A different Australia.

For me the change starts at Coolgardie which is a spot 3451 kilometres from Sydney and within spitting distance of Kalgoorlie and its naughty and distasteful delights. From there we drive gently, in style, down to Perth and then on to Fremantle to see the men of many nations play with their expensive aquatic toys. This port of Fremantle has been done over with great taste and style. The streets are clean. The atmosphere is exciting. We pull into the Sail and Anchor where they brew their own beer. A celebratory drink. Well earned, well appreciated. And then we drove home.

California driving

Driving in other countries is different. This is what happened when I drove to Monterey in California.

California, the State. San Francisco, the city. Monterey, the town. John Steinbeck, the author. For this Steinbeck fan, San Francisco is quite close to heaven. From San Francisco it is an easy drive down the peninsula to Santa Cruz and into Steinbeck territory.

I fly into San Francisco airport late in the afternoon. The signs are immediate America. 'No Ped Xing', 'Squeeze right', 'Occupation by more than 132 persons unlawful'. From Rent a Wreck I collect a Chevrolet Bel Air in two tones—cat-sick green and vile yellow. A veritable pimpmobile. And was it not in a car like this I drove into San Francisco for the 1967 Summer Of Love, to follow Timothy Leary's instructions to 'turn on, tune in, and drop out'? It was. And was it not in very much the same automobile I parked outside the City Lights Bookstore and went in and listened to Ginsberg recite *Howl* and got Jack Kerouac to sign my copy of *The Dharma Bums*? It was. This antediluvian American monster is the car of my youth. Be damned to the characterless compacts of today.

Now I drive across Highway 92 and its beguiling signs leading to San José along the Camino Real—the Royal Road. (Yes, I know the way to San José and a sterile, dreary city it is.

Fellow journalist John Sterlichhi, who lives there, swears it boasts a high school solely for pregnant schoolgirls. I almost believe it.)

Swing on to Highway 1, America's very own Pacific Highway, which takes me down the peninsula and along the coast, the rugged, rocky coast on the right, the remains of cypress forests on my left—and goes through Santa Cruz to Monterey. Coming back, I will use Highway 9 which is a backroad, in spite of the grandiose title, and follow the San Lorenzo river up, up into the Santa Cruz mountains and then through the magnificence of California redwoods in the Henry Cowell Redwoods State Park.

If I have enough time, on the way back I will stop at Felton on Highway 9 and ride on a steam train for an hour of nostalgia on the wondrously named Roaring Camp and Big Trees narrow-gauge railway line. No railway line of my youth ever swooped through stands of redwoods; it is true that only God could have made these trees, one of which is within spit of being a hundred metres tall. No train in the darkness of the Rhondda puffed like the Little Red Engine—I think I can, I think I can—up one of the steepest railway gradients in the world to Bear Mountain.

But that is on the morrow. Today is for blessed Monterey. Robert Louis Stevenson in travel-book mode wrote of Monterey in a fish-hook simile as being 'cosily ensconced beside the barb'. (At the time Stevenson was skulking around Monterey, waiting for the divorce of the light of his life, Fanny Osbourne.) Much earlier than Stevenson, Gaspar de Portola and the intrepid explorer for God, Father Junipero Serra, claimed Monterey for Spain and the Holy Catholic Church by establishing a fort and a mission in 1777. Now I claim it, yet again, for myself.

The sea as I drive down the coast road is white with rage and foam. Hurricane Gilbert has been creating havoc at sea and in Mexico. This is the dying fringe of the storm. Waves slam against the rocky coast and burst in white flags to mark the route ahead. I see no sea lions or seals as I did last year. Perhaps the sea is too rough. Perhaps they have a shelter where they hide from the big waves. Perhaps.

I am staying at the Monterey Bay Inn simply because of its address, 242 Cannery Row. From here, last night, I walked past the appalling tourist mockery that is Fisherman's Wharf—what sins are committed for the tourist dollar—and on to the Municipal Wharf at the end of Figuero Street. This is where the real fishing fleet is moored; where the buildings are properly dilapidated and the pelicans stalk the fish-smelling docks and landings. Pure Steinbeck.

Last night I dreamed I was Doc Rickett and that I still worked in my laboratory among the wonderful desperates of Cannery Row. This morning, over breakfast, I consider sadly the strong moral purpose that ran through all of John Steinbeck's Cannery Row novels. He was worried the major canning companies would, by dint of financial muscle, bully their way into ownership or control of all of the agricultural land in the area. Steinbeck was right to be worried. For that is what has come to pass.

Sad also to realise that the year Cannery Row was published, 1945, was the year the sardine fishing industry of Monterey died. As Steinbeck said at a later time: 'They are fishing for tourists now'. In the heyday of Monterey there were eighteen canneries, 100-odd fishing boats, 4000 workers, three gaudy brothels and a terrible smell of dead fish. Now, nearly all are gone.

Yet we can still see the old Cannery Row if we look with care. This morning I go to Foam Street, where the true Cannery Row starts, and look with pleasant melancholy at the rusted factories slowly collapsing, worn out by decades of effort to survive. I stand silently on the stone pilings of the deserted loading dock. It would have been better if I had delayed my visit by a couple of months. For this is the end of summer and the weather is still too warm, too pleasant for my mood. Cannery Row needs a touch of cold damp in the air for true dismal authenticity. And it is wrong that I should be here on a Saturday. Thursday, Sweet Thursday, is surely the only day to visit Monterey. But how can we change a business itinerary for literary requirements?

Much in Monterey remains the same, much has changed. La Ida Cafe of blessed memory is now Kalisa's, down from my hotel at 851 Cannery Row. Wing Chong Market has been transmogrified into the Old General Store (835 Cannery Row) and the building that once held Doc Rickett's Marine Lab still stands at 800 Cannery Row. Last time I was here it was a private club and I managed to smooth-talk my way in. This morning it seems sadly deserted. Do not confuse this, the genuine article, with Doc Rickett's Lab, a nightclub featuring country and western and rock 'n' roll bands which is at 85 Prescott Avenue, the sort of place Doc Rickett might have drunk at, but didn't.

When I have finished writing, I will stroll down to Sancho Panza for lunch. This restaurant is in an adobe building built in 1841 in Calle Principal—Main Street. There, in the crowded, low-ceilinged room, I will drink Mexican Corona beer with slices of lime and eat chile con carne con frijoles and remember John Steinbeck, the writer who gave me the smell, the feel, the reality of Monterey when I was a small boy in Wales.

17

Walking around

I walk down the Strand
With my gloves on my hand,
And I walk down again
With them off

W. F. Hargreaves, *Burlington Bertie*

It is a fact that not once in my life have I been out for a walk. I have been taken out for walks; but that is another matter.

Max Beerbohm, *Going Out for a Walk*

Walking takes me around the great cities of the world in style, and it saves me a lot of money as well. Consider London. There you can walk and be guided at the same time.

When I was young and ran a publishing company in London my offices were in Barnard's Inn. This is where Mr Pocket lived in *Great Expectations*. Around the corner was a group of buildings which had survived the Great Fire of London.

I mention this not to big-note, but to show that in London you cannot avoid history as long as you walk. Almost anywhere you care to stand you are near a major historical site. For London, more than any other city, is history. A lifetime is not enough to explore all of the facets of this great and historic city.

A traveller needs to be selective. My own way of seeing London—and I am still a tourist and explorer after all these

years—is on foot with a guided tour.

I am not, I must confess, that interested in modern London. Most modern architecture I find a blot and an excrescence (do architects' mothers know what their children do for a living?) Most modern pleasures pass me by. For me London, my London, is a wallow in history, not all of it sunshine and light.

For the first-time tourist, one of the quickest ways of getting your bearings is to go on one of the many guided walking tours. Here it pays to specialise.

The general tours basically consist of being stuck in a traffic jam in an open-topped bus while a guide makes fatuous remarks and juvenile jokes. The walking tours are something else again. They are normally led by knowledgeable types who are both eccentrics and fanatics—England breeds these people in abundance. You will learn more about London on one of these strolls through history than you ever will through reading a history book. For the full flavour, I recommend you do both—walk and tour first, read second.

One of the better collections of walks comes from City Walks and Tours which also appears to operate under the name of Walking Tours of London and Footprints Guided Walks. Here I speak from reasonably extensive experience. Typical price of a walk is £3, but there are season tickets which let you take as many walks as often as you want for £15. 50 a season.

My own favourite is the Dickens and Shakespeare walk

which starts on Sundays at 11.30 am and takes you back through history and fiction until you end up at the site of the old Globe Theatre. Then you have a quiet jar at the famous waterside pub, the Prospect of Whitby. Both civilised and educational. There are nineteen of these walking tours from this group alone and it is my ambition to go on every one.

A word of advice. All of the walking tours mentioned here take from one to three hours and they are never cancelled because of inclement weather. Forget fashion. Wear comfortable shoes. Always carry a small collapsible umbrella. I also carry a small hip flask in case of dire medical emergencies.

Rather more specialised are Cockney Walks, which again cost £3. I was never a lover of the idea of the London chirpy Cockney sparrow smiling in adversity. Indeed, I have often thought that the origin of the whingeing Pom idea came from Cockney immigrants. However, if you subscribe to the theory that London's unique character comes from the criminal elements who were born within sound of Bow Bells, these tours have a fascination all their own. It is just over one hundred years ago that London was shaken by the Jack the Ripper murders in which ladies of easy virtue were murdered and disembowelled in the lanes and alleyways of the East End.

I have always been happy to believe that these murders were done in the name of the Duke of Clarence, Queen Victoria's grandson, who had illicitly married and got a young lady up the duff. To make up your own mind, go on a ripper of a tour run by Streets of London and listen to Martin Fido, author of *The Crimes, Detection And Death Of Jack The Ripper* say, with great erudition but no certainty, what he thinks happened.

Continuing in that somewhat gruesome mode, Tragical History Tour—ah, what promise in that name—has an evening tour for a tenner which uses a bus, rather than your feet, to visit the various Ripper sites, plus the odd haunted house or two. Methinks they are stretching it a bit when they try and conjure up a phantom hitch-hiker in the Blackwall Tunnel. The tour very intelligently arranges to visit two pubs en route where you can sample the delights of real ale. This company also has full-day ghost-seeking tours, but in daylight some of the magic is missing.

If you feel you would rather be on your own, you can

construct your own tours. Now that I am an Australian, on this trip I decided I would try to discover what Australian connections could be found in London. I found there were far more than I had ever imagined.

James Cook lived at 88 Mile End Road in the East End and was married at St Margaret's Church in Barking. Captain Arthur Phillip was born in Bread Street, EC4. Sir Joseph Banks was born in Argyle Street in the West End and his house at 32 Soho Square was a centre for scientific research.

Just behind the square is a pub confusingly called The Coffee House which was one of the favourite Australian watering holes, 20 years ago. Now the pubs of choice are The King's Head in the Fulham Road, the Prince of Teck in Earls Court Road and The Greyhound in Fulham Palace Road.

To sort out a tour of Australia in London, the book to get is *Australian London* by Kate Murphy (Comerford and Miller). For me the essential handbook of London is *Everybody's Historic London* by Jonathan Kiek (Quiller Press) which has 20 tours described in loving detail. The tenth tour suggests you visit places with names which give the wondrous flavour of London to perfection.

Thomas More Street, Wapping Old Stairs, The Ratcliff Highway, Limehouse Causeway, St George-in-the-East and The Royal Mint. Walk these streets and visit with history. I was totally at ease with Dr Samuel Johnson when he wrote, 'When a man is tired of London he is tired of life; for there is in London all that life can afford'.

There is, true, a nasty air of parochial smugness there. (Johnson was also wrong on the subject of Scotland). But it is also true that no matter how often you visit London there is always something to explore, to visit, to enjoy.

For my taste, criminal walking in London is ever a great delight. That is not walking to commit crimes but walking places where crimes, real and imaginary, have been committed.

Jas Bowels has been my hero for many years. Sly, devious, indomitable, a mangler of the English language. He and his quite appalling son Rowley Boy are now part of my psyche. Jas Bowels was the creation of Margery Allingham, for me the foremost English crime fiction writer. Jas Bowels appeared in *More Work for the Undertaker*. In this minor masterpiece the self-effacing detective Albert Campion was brought in to investigate why members of the strange family Palinode were shuffling off this mortal coil at an unseemly rate. Like all good English detective novels the work intertwined an outrageously impossible plot with well observed workaday details.

True detective novels are very much an English scene although the genre has been exported to New Zealand and Australia. But not, in the full sense, to the United States. (Let not anyone write and mention Raymond Chandler for he was educated at Dulwich College in London.)

When I visit London, which is several times a year, I seem to see the place through the eyes of my favourite fictional characters of crime. Sadly the undertaking establishment of Jas Bowels and Rowley Boy is not traceable. It came full born from the mind of Margery Allingham although one could put forward the theory that it was somewhere near Islington. But other places in her other novels and those of other writers are there just for the looking. For me it is important to know that Albert Campion and his grotesque off-sider Magersfontein Lugg lived in Swallow Street, metamorphosed for fictional purposes into Bottle Street. Close to Piccadilly Circus. You can't miss it. Has its own police station.

Journalists used to come from Fleet Street, the Street of Fame or the Street of Shame, depending. Before you get to Fleet Street you can nip up to Bedford Row and at the end turn left into Sandland Street. This is where the publishing company of Barnabas had their offices in *Flowers for the Judge*. (There is a genuine Barnabas House but this is in Soho and there appears to be no connection.) While you are in that area stroll across to Holborn and then over to Staples Inn. It was here that Lord Peter Wimsey conferred with his solicitor, Mr Murbles, in *Clouds of Witness*, and stayed for lunch.

Fleet Street itself is full of fictional crime scenes but no longer journalists. Nowadays you do not see big name hacks tacking their way from the Pig and When and The Stab in the Back—two hostelries loved by English journos—returning to their offices to hammer out a few hundred words. These members of the press were like Salcombe Hardy who reported Wimsey's honeymoon in *Busman's Honeymoon* and is described by Sayers as being 'usually drunk.' The paper he worked on was the *Daily Yell* but in her books Dorothy Sayers also had the *Chronicle*— based on the *News Chronicle* for which I used to write—and the *Morning Star*.

When visiting Fleet Street start at the top at Temple Bar. Look down and remember Henry Lamprey describing the scene in *A Surfeit of Lampreys* by New Zealand author Ngaio Marsh.

Walk down Fleet Street and the building on the left which housed the *Daily Telegraph* was used by E. C. Bentley in *Trent's Last Case* as the publishing house for *The Record*. This was across the way from its sister evening paper *The Sun*. E. C. Bentley was once a leader writer on the *Daily Telegraph* and no doubt thought up many of his best plots while gazing into space. Leader writers have a lot of time to gaze into space. G. K. Chesterton placed *The Daily Reformer* in this building and, in fiction, a spineless editor wrote to the owner's directions. Chesterton himself had resigned from a newspaper rather than write to order.

If you are willing, for a moment, to move from matters temporal to matters spiritual you are just passing the church of St. Dunstan's where the Great Fire of London stopped and where John Donne was once vicar. Donne has gone as have the hacks of Fleet Street. He has gone to join the other metaphysical poets; they are dispersed to Fortress Wapping and hack behind barbed wire.

Across the road is El Vino's which is certainly the Pommeroy's Wine Bar to which John Mortimer had Rumpole repair after another triumphant bout in the courts. I never drank at El Vino's because the egocentric owner refused to serve women at the bar as if they were a lesser species. This may have changed but I cannot be bothered to check. That black glass and chrome building a little further down on the left hand side as you move down the hill used to house the *Sunday Express* which is where Dick Francis, surely the most competent of thriller writers living today, learned his trade writing a racing column. This after he had retired from racing where he had a magnificent career over the sticks.

Now turn left into Fetter Lane and pass the Printer's Devil (a relatively new pub) along Old Fetter Lane to an old pub called The Plough. Directly behind that is Barnard's Inn where I ran a publishing company for many years. Walk through the narrow alleyway at the end, turn right and continue until you come to the cast iron bridge over Holborn. This is where Margery Allingham once had an apartment and where she set St Peter's Square in *Tiger in the Smoke*. This, for my money, is her second best book. (*More Work for the Undertaker* with the lovely, lovely Mr Bowels being the best.)

And on and on it goes. You can tour the whole of London looking at either fictional crime spots or factual crime scenes. Or, in my case, a grisly mixture of both. Recently I went to lunch with two other journalists at L'Escargot in Soho. I took the tube to Oxford Street and came out into Argyle Street which houses The Palladium, the music hall of London. It was here that Robert Fentiman took Ann Dorland in Sayers's *The Unpleasantness at the Bellona Club*. It was to this theatre the landlady was given tickets in *The Train of Fu Manchu* by Sax Rohmer.

Then I cut across and walked down Carnaby Street where in *The Skull Beneath the Skin* by P. D. James, Cordelia Grey sent Bevis to get them lunch. I was now in Soho which has always been a good spot for crime. This is where rival gang leaders Jack Spot and Albert Dimes had their non-existent razor slashing contest. Non-existent by the time it got to the courts, that is. The area is still full of low life characters some of whom, sadly, are minor villains trying to be Soho characters and failing by a country mile. Manchester Freddy and Frank Norman—he of the razor scarred countenance—are, sadly, no longer with us.

Moving through Soho I walk through Soho Square and as I turn into Greek Street I pass the spot where 'Duds' Morrison—who came to a nasty end having his head booted in an alley—was involved in a fight in *Tiger in the Smoke*. On to the restaurant. I have heard it suggested that L'Escargot is housed in the 'evil-looking house' where Tommy Beresford bravely followed Boris in Agatha Christie's *The Secret Adversary*. I don't think so as there is supposed to be a small dilapidated square you can see from the windows. All I have ever seen are small dilapidated waiters.

Almost any step you take in London you will be surrounded by reminders of fictional or factual crime. London and crime go so well together. Does this mean that you may become a victim of a crime? It is not likely although I was nearly run over when walking backwards across Bond Street looking at Sotheby's which John Dickson Carr called Willaby's in *The Skeleton in the Clock*.

Avignon

It is not only in England that walking is the best way of sightseeing. The same is true of most, but not all, other cities. Regard, for the moment, Avignon.

Most of us know Avignon because of the bridge. As the song goes, 'Sur le pont, d'Avignon'. But there is much more to Avignon than the bridge which tries, but no longer succeeds, in crossing the Rhône.

First let us establish where Avignon is, get oriented. Avignon is in the department of Vaucluse which was founded in 1793. It was formed by bringing together the state of Avignon, the Comtat Venaisson belonging to the Pope, the principality of Orange, the Viguerie d'Apt and the county of Sault. Vaucluse is in Provence in the south of France. It lies between the two great valleys of the Rhône and Dorance and the lower foothills of the Alps. Nearby is the port of Marseilles and the Côte d'Azur.

Avignon spans a major crossroads for several countries which is why it is stamped with history. From Italy came first the Roman conquest, followed in the middle ages by the establishment of the Papacy at Avignon which effectively ruled the country until the revolution. Just listing the historical buildings within the small, walled confines of Avignon is too considerable a task for a single chapter. All I can give is a small sampling.

This morning, in Avignon, I went for a walk. Started with the church of St Agricol which was rebuilt in the fourteenth and fifteenth centuries—the legend is that the original was built in the seventh century by the saint himself—and contains an altar piece carved by Imbert Boachon who made this wondrous work somewhere around 1525. Out of the church and then down the narrow Rue Joseph Vernet to the Chapel de l'Oratoire which was built as a rotunda between 1730 and 1748. The interior is in the form of an ellipse opening on to six small chapels.

Further down the road to number 21 which was the house where Bonaparte wrote *Souper de Beaucaire*. Bonaparte spent a fair amount of time in Avignon and stayed at the Hôtel d'International on several occasions. Further down the same street, at number 7, is the Hôtel de Tonduti de Maloijac. This is not a hotel in our sense of the word but a town house with a Renaissance style tower.

Now left past the foot of the tower and on towards the Place Crillon. There, in front of me, is Avignon's first theatre, the Ancienne Comédie which was built in 1732 by Thomas Laînée. All around me is history. Over there, on my left, is the old Hôtel du Relais Royal where murders were committed during the White Terror of 1814. (Murder is a continuing theme in the buildings of Avignon. Medieval, ancient, even modern history has always demanded its sacrifices.)

On the other side is what was the Hôtel Amat de Graveson but is now the wholly admirable Hôtel L'Europe where Napoleon and many other luminaries stayed, including one of the Popes. Now it houses me.

Back into Rue St-Etienne where, at number 18, Joseph de Montgolfier first thought of the idea of using hot air to lift a balloon. From there I cut through Grande Fusterie and then through the city walls, for Avignon is a totally enclosed city, to one of the many bridges, Pont St Bénézet. This was started in 1177 and finished in 1185. This bridge was the first to span the Rhône and linked the 'territory of the Empire' to the 'territory of the Kingdom of France'. It was destroyed by the Rhône in flood. Now only four of the original 22 arches remain. There has been a lot of rain in the past few days and the Rhône is right up to its banks.

Now I turn back into the city and then up through the quarter called *La Balance* to the Palace of the Popes which was started by Pope Benedict XII between 1334 and 1342 and then added to, modified, extended over the centuries. This is quite the most amazing place and you can spend hours exploring the 18 000 square yards of buildings. I have. This time I visit the twelfth century cathedral of Notre Dame des Doms, view the quite splendid frescoes created by Simon Martini of Sienna and, on the far side of the chapel, see the tomb of Pope John XXII.

Still full of early morning energy, I climb to the top of the palace and view the surrounding countryside from a rooftop garden. Down again, now, to the secular streets and to the right is Le Petit Palais, the little palace that was built in the fourteenth century, later became a bishop's residence and now houses an art gallery of over 250 painting of assorted and ancient Italian schools as well as painting of the Avignon school that flourished from the twelfth to fifteenth centuries.

Starting to run out of steam and down Rue Jean Vilar, under the flying buttresses that support the Papal Palace. Then right and right again up to the Church of St Pierre which was built in the fourteenth century and modified in the sixteenth. The door and its two panels were carved by Antoine Votard in 1551. Inside the church, on a central pillar is a carving of the Vurgi, which is attributed to Jean Peru, one of the great artists of the 18th century.

Enough. I need my morning coffee. This is but one stroll through a small part of the streets of Avignon which I took quite early one morning in October. The sun was shining, the people of Avignon were having their coffee and croissants before starting the day's business and the world was at peace. Anywhere you walk within the walls of Avignon you will find beauty in the architecture, in the decoration, in the people, you will find history in the streets and you will find peace for your soul.

Bali

It is difficult to write about Bali without creating dissension. That parts of Bali have been altered, damaged, ruined, by Australian tourists there is no doubt, no debate, no discussion. But the sand, sun and sin strip around Kuta Beach is not, please believe me, the true Bali.

You do not have to follow the instructions of a travel brochure which says, I promise you, 'OK, you've come to Bali to sun, surf and rage. Understood'. And that from Garuda Indonesia, the country's own airline. When I go to Bali and see Kuta I always think of the Chinese description of Hong Kong. A pimple on the face of Mother China waiting to be squeezed. The same is true of the nastier tourist developments around Kuta.

The key to enjoying Bali is to realise that the average Australian tourist loses lower-limb mobility when overseas. Walk but ten paces away from the beaten track and you will be in another world, another country. You will be in Bali, as Nehru said, the morning of the world.

When I think of Bali—and I do, often—I think of it in four parts. First, the madding crowd's ignoble strife around Kuta Beach. Then the developments around Sanur Beach, which are fine if you want a holiday with good beach access at a cheapish price. Third, the Nusa Dua development which is international hotel style on a grand scale. You can stay there and make forays into the lifestyle of Bali.

Stay in any of these three places and you will very possibly, probably, have a holiday to suit your taste. But you need to move out to find, the fourth Bali, the real Bali—the morning of the world.

To find the real Bali travel out of the capital, Denpasar, literally the marketplace, and go up towards the mountains, towards the heart and soul of Bali.

First to Batubulan, a village that specialises in stone sculpture. You will see it offered at the roadside for sale. The volcanic stone, a pumice, is extremely soft and weathers very quickly. Just 200 metres away from the main road is the temple of Purta Puseh, which has, understandably, some of the finest carving in Bali. Wander there and enjoy them in peace. Most tourists do not walk this far. On now to Celuk, which is the silversmith's town. The speciality is filigree work with a fine and delicate air. Further on are the villages of Batuan, which produces some fine artists, and Sukawati, which is where the wind chimes that you will hear throughout Bali are made.

Balinese artists

There is a great tradition of painting in Bali. Before World War II, the Dutch artist Walter Spies went to stay in Ubud, of which more later, and he encouraged the locals to paint. Spies was shot by the Japanese during the war but the tradition remains. The flood of tourists has meant that any painting, by any Balinese, can be sold at a price. So you will see, sadly, hectares of unmitigated rubbish. Be patient. Smile a lot. Enquire. Eventually you will track down paintings, which are, in truth, great works of art.

As I write this I am looking at a masterpiece—the precise word—in yellow and brown and gold showing harvesters working in the rice fields. It has brought me peace and pleasure and solace for more than 20 years. Such art still exists in Bali, but you have to make an effort to seek it out.

Now we follow the fork of the road that takes us to Mas, which is a village devoted to woodcarving. Again there is a lot of fifth-rate stuff designed for the tourists, but here and there is an elegant piece with lines that flow like water. Search and be rewarded.

From Mas on to Ubud but, instead of taking the direct road, go up through Bedulu, past the Elephant Cave. All along our route there are temples. And always there are religious processions. My theory is that nature in Bali has always been so bountiful that supplying normal needs only takes an hour or two of work a day. Which leaves much time to devote to the Balinese version of Hinduism.

Ubud is an odd place. It was originally a very small village and its only claim to fame was that a senior prince, Tjokorda Agung Gede Sukawati, lived there in his palace—more like a collection of houses. The last time I saw the prince alive he was shopping in Coles in Bondi wearing three woollen cardigans and a contented smile. Dead now. Had an amazing funeral.

When I first went to Ubud it had one roadside eating place, a *warung*, and kerosene lamps. Now there is a bitumen road, street lights, telephones and cars. Ubud has an art gallery, the Puri Lukisan Museum of Modern Art, which contains some of the best work of the great Balinese artists. Go there first to get your eye in and then you will be able to work your way quickly through the schlock that you will be offered, to the treasures beyond.

Now walk out of Ubud, across the bridge, up the hill towards Sajan. Now move off the main road. Wander along the tracks through the fields. The tourists start to disappear. The people call and smile at you. The trees sweep across the road giving a welcome shade. There, over on the left, is a small temple. And beyond, a tree decorated because, in Bali, every tree has its day.

Coming down the road towards you is a procession of pure beauty and style. The women of Bali carrying offerings— intricate works of art created from flowers and rice and fruit—and walking in a stately procession towards the temple. Solomon in all his glory did not boast a retinue such as these.

Now, over to the right, the landscape opens and the emerald rice terraces of Bali cascade down to the Campuan river and then soar again up the opposite hillside. Below, the villagers are bathing in the river and, to your right, a young boy is herding a flock of ducks which are, true, marching in step. A magic trick. But this is all magic. The magic of Bali. Go there, off the beaten track, and experience it for yourself.

Frankfurt

The tourism people have put together a 60-minute walking tour of Frankfurt which works extremely well.

Start at the Fountain of Justice and walk past the Frankfurt Town Hall and the medieval half-timbered houses. Then, past the art exhibition—Frankfurt is the art capital of Germany—and historical gardens and on to the cathedral. From there, more art exhibitions and art galleries.

On to St Nicholas' Church and then down the road to the historical museum which has a splendid coin collection. Across to the Haus Wertheim, which is a magnificent half-timbered building. Follow the banks of the River Main to a medieval tower, and on to St Leonard's Church. Then you go through a narrow alley until you arrive at the Carmelite monastery. That is not far from Goethe's birthplace.

The tour then stops at what was once a garden house but is now a café, and moves on to St Catherine's Church before ending at Paul's Church, Pauliskirche, which often has been called the cradle of German democracy. A quick way to see what Frankfurt has to offer.

Hong Kong

Let me try to show you another Hong Kong, my Hong Kong. A Hong Kong that is closer to the truth. Start off very early one morning and come with me up to Bowen Road. This is about a third of the way up the Peak on the Hong Kong side. Bring your walking shoes.

Bowen Road is absolutely level and runs for four kilometres between Magazine Gap Road and Wanchai Gap Road. You start by wending your way between some of the high-rise blocks of apartments that cost an arm and a leg to rent. Full of prosperous Chinese and *gwailos*—the not unkindly Cantonese term for foreigners, meaning 'white ghost'.

Then, after a few hundred metres, there is a small park in which there will be dozens of people practising tai chi. This is not a martial art: it is a series of interlinked movements that stretch the sinews, relax the mind and slow the heart beat. Pass the park and then Bowen Road becomes closed to cars and motorbikes. You are now among groups of walkers striding along Bowen Road to greet the new day. Among them are elderly gentlemen taking caged birds for a walk.

The Chinese do not like selling budgies and canaries to Europeans. They are of the opinion that we are cruel to them because we do not take them for walks. Underneath each cage is a handle. When two of the gentlemen meet, they will hold their cages on high by this handle so that the birds can talk to each other, while the owners also enjoy an early morning conversation. Suddenly, on your left appears a view of the grand and glorious harbour of Hong Kong. For more years than I care to remember, I walked this path every morning and the view never failed to move me. Continue along the path. At the halfway mark, there is an elderly lady selling Chinese tea. Bid her a formal good morning—*jo san*—and then pass on.

What are those flames ahead? People worshipping their ancestors by lighting joss sticks.

As you move along, the path starts to fill with the early morning walkers, the dawn joggers. There is jostling, no pushing. All is smiles and friendly greetings. You begin to feel that you have become part of an extended family. Down to the left, there is a badminton court and although it is not yet fully light, there are young people playing there. The people of Hong Kong are sports crazy.

On now, till we reach the end and look with wonder at a serpentine fly-over that hangs in space. A group of English engineers made a study of this corner some years ago and wrote a long and learned report explaining why the fly-over would be impossible to build. The Chinese builders, knowing nothing of these matters, built one anyway.

Now take a bus or a taxi down to Central. Walk through the gardens by Statue Square under the gaze of the Hilton. Again, there will be serious Chinese going through the gentle movements of tai chi.

Carry on until you come to the Mandarin Hotel—Man Wah jau din in Cantonese—where the coffee shop serves one of the best breakfasts in the civilised world. The service is quiet, restrained and elegant. After breakfast, walk under the tunnel by the side of the Mandarin and then turn left along the waterfront to the Outlying Ferries Pier. There is a choice of ferries going to all the islands of Hong Kong. Today, we will go to Lantau. Once, I lived there.

Lantau has a land area twice that of Hong Kong island and a population of about 20 000, which is why it is peaceful and serene. Take the ferry to Silvermine Bay, which will give you a gentle and pleasant ride. As you travel, watch the water-borne activity, for Hong Kong is a harbour and lives as a great seaport.

At Lantau, take the bus to the bright red-and-gold Po Lin monastery. After a vegetarian lunch served by the monks, walk round the Shek Pik reservoir. You are—believe me, for this is true—in the countryside. The countryside of China. There will be no one, no one, to interrupt your thoughts. No push, no rush, no jostle. It is not widely publicised or known that about three-quarters of Hong Kong is countryside, not city. Then wend your way back to get the ferry once more to Hong Kong.

As you travel, talk to the Cantonese people. When they are not pressured for time, they are among the most courteous in the world. They will try their English on you with some hesitation, for they fear being laughed at. Act pleasantly, listen, smile a lot and you will be treated for what you are. An honoured visitor. A guest of Hong Kong.

New York

Except in the morning and evening rush hours, dirty, ill-maintained and badly driven taxis are plentiful with $1. 50 for flagfall and then the turbo-charged meter starts topping it up. If you have any problems with a cabbie, take his number and report the incident to the Taxi Commission on 869 4110. Some of my New York friends know this number by heart.

The subways are fast and cost a dollar a trip. Rather you than me on some sections. I am assured you can hire a car and drive it yourself, but I have never been game.

Mostly, in New York, no matter what the weather, I walk. Difficult to get lost in Manhattan. Basically a grid with First, Second, Lexington, Third, Park, Fifth, Sixth (now somewhat grandly called the Avenue of the Americas) and Seventh running north–south and numbered streets running east–west with Broadway a diagonal slash across the middle. It gets confused down around Greenwich Village. I am a solitary person, so I frequently walk by myself but, on occasion, I go on a guided walk organised by New York Walkabout which has 25 different tours. I can also speak highly of those from the 92nd Street YMCA, which offers weekend tours.

The streets of New York are a constant variety show.

You will need a map even though most of New York is laid out in a logical fashion. Once you have nutted it out you will never get lost.

Do not ask a policeman for directions. I once did. He was a mountainous member of New York's finest who looked, in his wet rain slickers, like Darth Vader with a baseball club in his hand. I said I would like to get to the Berkshire Hotel. He replied: 'I'm not stopping you, buddy.' New York, in this respect, is totally unlike London.

If you start at the southern tip of Manhattan Island—and for me, New York is Manhattan Island and all other places are outside the law—you begin at Battery Park. From here you can catch the Staten Island ferry which is one of the great sightseeing trips of the world.

To the east is the Fulton Fish market and American publisher Rupert Murdoch's *New York Post*. Move along and you will find the South Street Seaport museum outside which is moored sailing ships and other delights. Just to the north is Wall Street. Around here there is no logic in the streets, but a fascinating maze. Through the maze you find the World Trade Centre and from the top, 107 floors up, you can see the whole of Manhattan spread out below you.

As you move up from the World Trade Centre you leave the financial district of New York and move into what might be thought of as the government district. Brooklyn Bridge, still for sale to eager mug punters, is to the east. City Hall, which you cannot fight, is in a convenient clump with other government buildings.

At the north-east end is Mott Street of which Ella Fitzgerald sang, 'Tell me what street, compares with Mott Street in July'. This is Chinatown where the language of the streets is Cantonese and Mandarin—with a little Yiddish added for flavour.

Now we come to Tribeca which stands logically for Triangle Below Canal, and was once a cheapish place to rent an apartment. Above and to the west is SoHo which is capitalised that way because it is South of Houston Street—pronounced House-ton. Trendy.

Moving up on the east side above Chinatown we come to Little Italy and then to Greenwich Village.

Up now through Gramercy Park, expensive and stylish, through 23rd Street and the fur district. Pass Penn Station on your left which is part of Madison Square Garden and into the garment district where you will be run over by trolleys laden with shmutter. Now, there is the Empire State Building and this is Broadway and over there is Macy's and a short walk away is Fifth Avenue.

Eat your meals as you walk. New York is a town of street eating, street food. This is, I promise you, the biggest outdoor buffet in the world. Philadelphia steak sandwiches, sashimi, turkey hamburgers, satay, hot roti goat, sushi, tacos, fried chicken with jalapeno sauce, rolls in a wondrous variety, falafel, sausage heroes, gyros, foot-long frankfurters, pizza, vichysoisse, Acapulco salads, shish kebab, burritos, shrimp Parmesan, tortillas, ice cream in 50 flavours, chocolate covered Oreos. Wash it down with assorted colas, coffee, milk or the world's most dreadful tea.

Who needs restaurants?

Rome

Walk with me around the glory that was Rome. Ignore, for the moment, St Peter's. That takes a full day with at least an hour, perhaps more, regarding the frescoes of Michelangelo. Instead, come with me quite early one morning to the Forum.

Come in from the via dei Fori Imperiali just behind the Vittorio monument. Believe for the moment that it is, indeed, the tomb of the city's founder, Romulus. And then past the Palace of Domitian to the Colosseum that was erected by Emperor Titus. Forget the usual old cobblers that this was where Christian martyrs died. They did not. Wild animals did—on opening day 5000 of them were slaughtered. So did pagan gladiators; men who died in the games for the entertainment and edification of the citizens of Rome. In the quiet still of the morning you can hear, echoing down the years, *Ave, Imperator, morituri te salutant.*

Now to the Pantheon which was built in 120 AD as a monument to all the gods. It is still standing because it was consecrated as a church. Think not that it was the barbarians that destroyed ancient Rome. It was the Christians.

On to the 200-year-old Spanish Steps in the Piazza di Spagna. Let us try to get there before the buskers have arrived, before the smart-suited non-passionate travellers start arriving at the American Express offices opposite the steps.

In the centre of the Piazza is Bernini's Fountain of the Barcaccia (which sounds romantic until you find that in English it means the Old Boat). At the bottom of the steps is the Keats and Shelley Memorial House where these poets once lived. It's now a museum.

Time now to stop and take a coffee and watch the people.

On another day go to St Peter's and the Vatican. Every visitor to Rome will visit the Vatican—the heart of the Catholic Church. Again, take it slowly, *festina lente.* This is Rome and she is a dignified lady who will not be hurried. Take each sight as it comes. You always can go back again. And again.

Start with the Belvedere Courtyard—full of classical sculpture and, especially, the Apollo Belvedere and Laocoon. The Raphael rooms, the Sistine Chapel with that masterpiece of a ceiling by Michelangelo painted to the greater glory of God. And on and on and forever on.

Enough for the moment. Let us leave the religious and return to the secular. Sometimes Rome, with its shops and its architecture, its restaurants and its traffic becomes too much. Head for the decompression chamber of Tivoli, an hour or so outside the city. The sixteenth-century Villa d'Este is a park of waterfalls, small and large, a park of fountains, simple and ornate. The house and gardens are tranquil and quiet. An oasis of peace.

Then, refreshed, back to Rome to the basilicas of Santa Maria Maggiore—all gilt mosaics and woodwork—and of San Giovanni in Laterano, the cathedral of Rome.

Samoa

We are in Apia, in Western Samoa. Come for a walk with me in the early morning.

We are staying at the Tusitala Hotel in Apia, the capital of Western Samoa. First we have breakfast overlooking the pool and, inevitably, the manager eases over to make sure that everything is perfect. In paradise one expects perfection.

Now out from the hotel and cross Mulinu'u Road. If we turned left we would be going up to the observatory and Mulinu'u Point. Along that road we would find the memorial to the sailors who lost their lives in the great hurricane of March 16, 1889. On that day there were seven warships moored in Apia Bay: three German, three American and one British. Only the British ship, *Calliope*, escaped. The German *Eber*, *Adler* and *Olga* and the American *Trenton*, *Nipsic* and *Vandalia* were sunk and 130 sailors lost their lives. There would have been many more deaths if the Samoans, led by Seumanu, chief of Apia, had not taken their boats into the teeth of the hurricane and through the surf to the rescue.

Today we will not be going to Mulinu'u Point. Instead, we will turn right and head towards the town of Apia. It is quite early in the morning and the sun has not gained any bite for the day ahead. We are going to walk right along the waterfront until we get to another hostelry, Aggie Grey's, where we will have morning tea.

Before we start, look to the right along the bay. It is much as it has been for the past century. The open air market, over there on the left, has not changed dramatically. Further down on the right we will come to the court house which is pretty much the same. What has changed is the road and the traffic. Before the turn of the century this road was cut by several streams, almost rivers, coming down from the hills. Many of them were bridged by planks and primitive drawbridges. For example, next to the Mulivai Catholic church, which we will be passing later on, the Mulivai Stream comes out to the sea. This used to be crossed by a 30 centimetre-wide plank which was often missing. Now there is a relatively smooth highway swinging right around the fringes of the bay.

Probably the first European to see the bay was the Dutch

navigator Jacob Roggewein who was followed closely by de Bougainville in 1758 and La Perouse in 1787. The arrival of La Perouse caused a nasty incident. The best information is that the French explorers attacked and killed a Samoan who was suspected of petty theft. In the retaliatory attack that followed, over a dozen crew from the French ship were killed. This gave the Samoans a reputation that was totally undeserved. They were regarded in Europe as a savage, warrior-like race that would attack without warning. It was not for several decades that this erroneous impression was erased.

The Beach Road that we see ahead of us has always been the main thoroughfare of Apia. The original market building, over there to the left, was presented to the people by Herr Kunst, a wealthy German gentleman who lived in what was then German Samoa at the turn of the century. The market hall runs in very much the same way now as it did then. The smells, the sounds, are much the same. The never-empty Kava bowl, with its circle of regulars, has been there since time immemorial. The vegetables and fruits laid out for sale are much the same.

What has changed are the trucks pulled up outside and the absence of pigeons. For many centuries pigeons abounded in Samoa and were part of the staple diet. Then, just after the turn of the century, the vast majority of them disappeared. There are still some around, but they are few and far between. The first building on our left after the Apia bowling club is WSTEC which was originally the head office of DH and PG, a German trading company that for years was the biggest in Samoa.

There was originally a major complex of buildings and the whole area was owned by the company. This company was inextricably involved in the history of Samoa and one of the clerks was directly involved in a great rebellion which ended with Apia being shelled. The other major trading company was run by the redoubtable H.J. Moors, an American who spent his life in Samoa. The German influence in Samoa cannot be underestimated. It is the popular image that the Germans were rough, harsh colonisers. This may have been the case in parts of Africa. Not so in Samoa where their conduct appears to have been benign and beneficent.

Back to our stroll. As far as can be made out, almost opposite the market, but closer to the Tusitala, was a cottage where lived

Mrs Bully Hayes and her children. Bully Hayes was the roughest, toughest blackbirder in the South Pacific and was known and feared throughout the islands. There was only one person of whom Bully Hayes was afraid, his wife. Every time he came ashore, she gave him the rounds of the kitchen. These set battles were a widely appreciated form of entertainment in Apia. Bully Hayes was one of a long line of South Sea island toughs based in Western Samoa who had names that sang, Paunchy Billy, Sweet William, Charley Squarehead, Bill the Steward, Cranky Jack, Flash Harry Smith, Sam Slick and Jimmy the Bush Fowl.

Bully Hayes was a big man and looked, according to contemporary reports, like a defrocked bishop. In 1879, Bully Hayes was killed when he had his head bashed in with an iron tiller handle on board his ship *Lotus*. No one was ever charged with the killing.

Somewhere near that building, towards the turn of the century, was the Russian Bear Public House which was kept by Charley the Russian, no other name is known. He sold gin at two shillings a large bottle and one shilling for a small bottle which held over a pint. The gin was always watered down. Charley never bathed and never changed his only two pieces of clothing a shirt and a pair of dungarees. He could speak several European languages. It was at the Russian Bear Public House that most of the crew of the American battleship Lackawanna arrived some time in 1884. They had not been ashore for several months and had serious amounts of money in their possession. Many of these sailors were enticed by young Samoan maidens to do a runner and join them in villages on the far side of the island. These deserters were then offered back by the chiefs of the villages to the commander of the ship at $13 a head. After the deal was made, the deserters were escorted back after being hog tied by the Samoans. This and similar episodes of earning money through enticed desertion had a strong financial impact on Samoa. This particular example of negative-nooky-gearing, for example, brought in some $90 000 to the economy of Samoa.

A few years later, on the shore directly opposite, a Chinese trader named Ah Wing built a full-size junk. No one was willing to sail her except for a beachcomber called Flash Harry Smith. The junk was loaded and Flash Harry set off on a trading trip of the nearby islands. The boat was totally unseaworthy and averaged less than a kilometre a day. Eventually, it was poled back over the reefs and sank outside the Chinaman's store. It was this same Ah Wing who had a catastrophic fire in his warehouse. Local residents were ready to rush in and save his goods but Ah Wing protested that they should not risk their skins. The store burnt to the ground and there seemed a very small amount of rubble for the amount of goods that were supposed to have been in store.

As we move further down the road we will come to a row of nightclubs and restaurants. The nightclubs are not nightclubs as you and I know them. More like serious drinking bars with canned, and sometimes live, music added. Again this is not much changed as in 1876, H. J. Moors, the great Samoan trader, wrote: 'Six public houses, with their accordions and organs, kept up considerable noise until all hours'.

In the 1870s, just past where the Catholic church is now, there was a boarding house and restaurant kept by Ah Sue and Manila Joe A'Costa where a meal was two shillings and a room the same price. It was in a rooming house very much like this, but on the other Samoa, that the irrepressible and sinful Sadie stayed in Somerset Maugham's novel *Rain*.

Again, just past the Catholic church, about where Otto's Reef now stands, was the Eagle Hotel. Writing of it in 1882, H. J. Moors reported: 'On the inland side stood the disreputable Eagle Hotel, kept by a scoundrel known as Black Bill Henry who maintained a company whose nightly frolics attracted a large number of sailors and others, and many hold-ups and robberies took place along that narrow road'.

Now we come past the John Williams Memorial. If we turn inland we will come to Vailima, the home of Robert Louis Stevenson. Stevenson Tusitala, the teller of tales loved Samoa and the Samoans with a passion. When he died, a track was hacked overnight to the top of the hill behind his home and his body buried by his friends, the Samoans. The tomb is still there with its timeless inscription,

Under the wide and starry sky,
Dig the grave and let me lie,
Glad did I live and gladly die,
And I laid me down with a will.

This be the verse you grave for me:
Here he lies where he longed to be;
Home is the sailor, home from sea.
And the hunter home from the hill.

On another occasion we will scramble up that hill and pay our respect to that great writer, R. L. S, who so loved Samoa and the Samoans.

For now we head on along the coast and arrive at our destination, Aggie Grey's. This hotel became an institution during World War II when American troops used it as a base camp. They thronged there, it was said, for the hamburgers. There may, of course, have been a considerable number of non-licentious soldiery stationed in Apia to whom a real hamburger would have been an irresistible attraction. One feels, however, that there might have been other attractions with sly grog being well to the fore. Sadly, a few years ago, the redoubtable Aggie went to her reward, although her grand-daughter, Aggie Grey reborn, is still very much in evidence. The frenzied days of the war in the Pacific are now well past. These days Aggie Grey's is a respectable modern South Pacific hotel with stunning South Seas architecture and a possibly disreputable past.

18

Camping

Those who have never dwelt in a tent have no idea either of the charm or of the discomfort of a nomadic existence. The charm is purely romantic, and consequently very soon proves to be fallacious.
Victoria Sackville-West, *Twelve Days*

Australians travelling to Europe often find on arrival that hotel charges bite far deeper into their budgets than expected. Prices ranging upwards from $50 a night for very average double rooms can drain resources quickly, leaving little for travelling and spending. An alternative to the high cost of hotels, particularly for friends planning to travel together around the Continent, is hiring a car and, in summer, staying at camp sites.

Europeans are fond of the outdoors and there are camp sites wherever people holiday. Eurocamp, a subsidiary of the Next group of clothing stores, has 104 sites in France, West Germany, Spain, Yugoslavia, Belgium, Luxembourg, Italy and Austria. Many are away from the population centres in the Swiss Alps, the French Riviera, Tuscany, Innsbruck and the German Black Forest, but Eurocamp also has sites in Florence, Paris and Munich.

Although some sites are accessible by public transport, Eurocamp is primarily intended for motoring holidays and is particularly suited to the Australian tradition of buying cheap cars and vans in London, travelling around Europe and selling the vehicle before heading home. Eurocamp provides a choice of six-berth tents or six-berth caravillas, which appear to be of a very high standard.

The caravillas (9.5 m long by 2.5 m wide) and tents (5.2 m by 4.9 m) all come with cooking facilities, pots, pans, crockery and cutlery. The caravillas have showers and toilets. Both forms of accommodation include a double bed and four single beds, all fully sprung, and it is possible for a group of three couples to request three double beds.

Eurocamp bases its charges on a minimum of two adults with all children under fourteen years included in the price, except in high season (July 16–August 31) when they are charged $6 a night.

In the high season a couple would pay $125 a night for a caravilla, with each extra adult being charged $12 so six friends holidaying together would pay $28.80 each. In the budget season (September 1–15) the price for a couple drops to $70 and for extra adults to $8 so six sharing would pay $17 each. Before June 14 and after September 16 the cost is less than $14 each per night. Tents are considerably cheaper. Six sharing a tent in budget season paying only $12 each and even in high season only $22.20. Australians, who generally make the visit to Europe worthwhile by staying several weeks, also benefit from a price reduction for bookings longer than nineteen days.

The campsites come with a variety of amenities—most have restaurants, bars and either a swimming pool, lake or beach, and are in areas of scenic beauty, historic interest, wine-producing areas or with sporting facilities. Some of the French campsites have all of the above. All campsites have running hot and cold water, modern washing facilities and fresh water taps close to the tents.

Many of the sites are in France, in the Loire Valley, Dordogne, Riviera, Provence, Pyrenees, Brittany, Normandy and Picardy, with an exhaustive list of scenic and culinary attractions.

The biggest attraction must be the free childcare, which is provided at about half the camp sites. Eurocamp marketing director, Julian Rawel, says families can leave their children with trained childcare officers while they explore places of historic interest, go hiking or venture into town for a romantic dinner. Most sites also have children's play areas.

Mr Rawel says Eurocamp is the Holiday Inn of camping—the caravillas may all look the same, but uniform standards means that customers know what they are getting at each site. Each camp site has resident English-speaking staff.

There are on-site discos, speciality nights and dances as well as indoor games and a range of group sports activities. A number of camp sites, depending on location, have either sailboards or canoes, which are included in the accommodation charge.

Eurocamp also provides complete touring guides to Europe with every booking. These are particularly useful and although intended to help you find the camp site, include a good road atlas of Western Europe (in colour with overlapping pages), local guide books and excellent local road maps.

Eurocamp is represented in Australia by Walkabout Travel. Its Sydney office is at 5 Angel Place; phone 2312644 or (008) 3221629 toll-free.

19

Health

Exercise is bunk. If you are healthy, you don't need it: if you are sick you shouldn't take it.

Henry Ford

Look to your health; and if you have it, praise God, and value it next to a good conscience; for health is the second blessing that we mortals are capable of; a blessing that money cannot buy.

Izaak Walton, *The Compleat Angler*

The chances of your being taken sick while travelling are higher than your chances of being taken sick while staying at home. This is because infections and bugs to which your body has not built up resistance are lurking at your destination. Being taken sick on holiday can be utterly depressing because you have done your time off and your dough.

I am not claiming great expertise in this area—I have no medical training, just unfortunate experience. Last year I caught typhus in Africa. And it was my own fault. These are the things I believe you can do to stay relatively healthy while you travel.

Vaccinations

Healthy travel is a question of balancing the risks. On most holiday jaunts, the chances of getting seriously ill are small, the

need for vaccinations minimal, the amount of medications you should carry, minute. The more adventurous you are as a traveller, the more you stray off the beaten track, the greater the risks.

Until recently, travellers had to depend on the advice of general practitioners on how to deal with these risks. Doctors frequently lacked expertise in these areas. For example, my doctor had never been beyond Fiji and was not quite sure of the geographical location of Zaire. A private company, Medical Advisory Services for Travellers Abroad (MASTA), has been set up to give all the medical advice needed for anyone travelling abroad.

I was ever suspicious of organisations like MASTA and I approached it with all my prickles raised. In this, I was wrong. MASTA is the genuine article. The company is associated with the Australian tropical health program at the University of Queensland and is connected with a similar program that has been running in Britain for the past five years which is, in turn, associated with the London School of Tropical Medicine. MASTA is also associated with the communicable diseases section of the Department of Health in Canberra and the Centre for Disease Control in Atlanta, Georgia, in the US. It has, then, semi-official status although, I stress, it is a private organisation which is run as a profit-making enterprise.

MASTA offers three levels of advice: a non-personalised

service for a short trip; a fairly serious in-depth report for a long trip; a total study if you are going to live for a time in a new country. Prices for the reports are $25, $50 and $75 respectively. Within that price, six destinations can be included.

Let us take a specific example of how MASTA works. Recently, I went to Zimbabwe. Before going, I chose the middle level of medical advice from MASTA, as I thought I would be travelling around Zimbabwe a fair amount but not living there.

First, I had to give MASTA some information about my general health, my various inoculations and vaccinations. MASTA then printed out for me a personalised report that ran for 16 closely typed pages. The report provided every scrap of information I needed to make my trip to Zimbabwe as trouble-free as possible. It warned about the dangers of malaria in the Zambezi Valley in the north of the country and spelt out, in great detail, what I should do about it. The report also gave much valuable advice as to what I should do if, after having taken all precautions, I had an attack of malaria. Speaking from personal experience—I have had several attacks of what they laughingly call 'benign' malaria—I thought all the advice solid and soundly based.

There was supplementary good advice on other possible problems and lots of dos and don'ts. It even covered AIDS, informing me that, in Zimbabwe, 119 cases had been officially reported and that there were 321 unofficial cases. It added that 'casual sexual intercourse is very risky'. That is now an international truth.

If you are going abroad and you are not certain of the risks, I would think $50 spent with MASTA would be a worthwhile investment. If I had been able to call on its advice before my last trip to Africa, I would not have contracted typhus, which was not a pleasant experience.

Vaccinations are tricky things. The common notion that a few little jabs will act as a magic force-field, warding off all germs, is simply not true. Cholera vaccination is a good example. The World Health Organisation (WHO), the body which oversees vaccinations and epidemic control worldwide, is actively discouraging cholera vaccinations because the vaccine is not a particularly effective one, especially in epidemics. MASTA, in its reports, says precisely the same thing.

Generally, the number of vaccinations required is declining. The world is now considered smallpox free. General practitioners will offer most of the inoculations needed for travel, although they may require advance notice to obtain the necessary vaccines. The Department of Health is the authority to consult when it comes to vaccinations and runs an information line for GPs to keep abreast of the latest developments. The only inoculation offered by the Department of Health is against yellow fever, as it is a disease that still requires quarantine—part of WHO policy. This vaccination is mandatory if you are travelling to central Africa or parts of South America.

Some countries require certain vaccinations for quarantine, as well as for health reasons. For instance, you cannot travel from India to Pakistan without a cholera stamp on your international health certificate. Such mandatory quarantine restrictions vary with each country.

Optional vaccinations are a matter of balancing the advantages against the disadvantages. Dr Peter Vodicka, a medical officer with the Department of Health, believes hygiene, and being careful with food and drink, are at least as important as having the correct vaccinations, and says that if travellers are staying in up-market hotels, they need only a minimum of inoculations.

A typhoid vaccination is worthwhile because it is very effective with minimal side-effects. 'As well as having a typhoid shot, anti-malaria tablets should always be taken in areas of high risk,' he says. 'Malaria is a nasty disease and, unfortunately, quite easy to catch.'

If you have children, the story is slightly different. Infants under 12 months of age need no vaccinations, but children over 12 months require the same vaccinations as adults. Anti-malaria tablets can be a bit tricky. At least one of the brands is not recommended for children, so check with your doctor.

Many vaccinations, such as the meningitis, tetanus and polio boosters and the gamma-globulin shot against hepatitis, are optional and should be discussed with your doctor. They are only absolutely essential, according to Dr Vodicka, for travellers who intend to rough it.

If you are travelling to Europe, North America or Japan, you will not need to have any vaccinations at all.

Flying

When flying, cut down on the booze and the food. I always think it very sad that the airlines go out of the way to create great dishes to tempt you in-flight, when the ideal situation is that you should cut back on what you eat, not eat more. Although I am not a vegetarian, I register as one with most airlines I use, simply because I find I stay healthier that way.

Cutting down on the alcohol is even better sense. The pressurisation of the cabin appears to increase the speed with which the alcohol gets to the brain. The dryness of the cabin dehydrates you, so that you want to drink more. The free champagne is a terrible temptation. Drink too much of it and you end up with a vicious headache and an incipient hangover. If you must drink, dilute the effect with plenty of soda water to help alleviate the dehydration.

Don't forget the kaolin, preferably with morphine. Variously called Montezuma's revenge, the green apple two-step, the running screaming diabolicals, Delhi belly, Malta dog and the dreaded lurgy, diarrhoea can strike at any time, but especially at the beginning of a holiday. It is often not the result of a bug or infection. The reason is more likely to be a change in environment, different and exotic foods, an excess of booze and late nights. On holidays, the idea is that you should take it easy.

If you should be stricken, the sovereign cure on which I have depended all my life is kaolin clay suspended in a mixture. It used to be available mixed with morphine, but that is now illegal without a prescription. I once ministered to a helpless band of visitors on a Fiji island through a long Christmas weekend. The kaolin mixture worked every time. Add to this starvation, plenty of fluids and lots of rest. Remember, as it says in the Bible, this too shall pass.

Note that if you are taken seriously ill immediate medical treatment is essential. As I was editing this piece a friend of mine called to say he had just been severely ill in Tokyo after eating a crab meat salad on the airline flying him there. The only answer was to get a doctor as quickly as possible. In fact, he needed an injection just to control the stomach cramps. Kaolin and morphine does nothing for that sort of ailment. When in doubt, see a doctor.

Take an adequate supply of your prescribed medicines with you. Your medicine may be sold under a different name or a different formula overseas. It may be hard, even impossible, to get. It is also possible, in some Asian countries, to be sold bogus medicines that may actually harm you. You must carry a prescription with you to show you are a legitimate user (even codeine in some countries is considered a dangerous drug). The Federal Department of Health recommends travellers make a note of the generic names of any regular medication they have to take and, if they wear glasses, of the prescription. Some may feel this is going a bit too far.

Have all the essential jabs carried out in plenty of time. But only have those injections you know are absolutely and legally necessary.

For malaria there are anti-malarial tablets, but if misused these can be as dangerous as the disease itself. No medication is 100 per cent effective. Personally, I try to avoid all areas that have malaria so that I don't need to take any pills. If I am in mosquito territory I take obsessive and traditional precautions against being bitten.

If you suffer from travel sickness, get a prescription from your doctor. Note that many of the standard remedies like hyoscine and antihistamine can cause drowsiness—a bit of a worry if you are going to be driving or conducting serious business shortly after arriving.

Take a day off before you go and a day off after you return. Travel is tiring. Starting journeys fagged out means that you are extremely susceptible to illness and injury. When you come back from your holiday you will need at least 24 hours to recover.

Make sure you are fully insured for medical disasters. I cannot emphasise this enough. Health insurance, which is covered in another chapter, is vital in places like the United States and Switzerland, where medical expenses can very easily exceed $1500 a day. Medicare does not cover you when you are abroad. Nor do most medical funds. You need special cover.

If you have a heart problem carry a copy of your ECG.

Don't drive, and stay intact. Most tourist accidents are caused by driving. The simple answer is not to. Many countries in Asia will provide a chauffeur-driven car almost for the same price as a self-drive hire. Avoid motor cycles at all costs.

Jet lag

This is the problem. It used to be that sailing ships, and later liners, went through time zones at a stately pace so that everyone had time to adjust. In the early days of flying the large number of stops between, say, England and Australia, forced a regime of rest, fly, rest. Now we can fly to almost anywhere in Europe with one stop. Under those conditions jet lag can possibly, probably, certainly set in.

It is caused because on long travel sectors, like London to Sydney, you fly through ten time zones. The result is that the natural body rhythm which tells us when to wake up, when to eat, when to go to the loo, is thrown totally out of synchronisation. The results, depending on the age and the metabolism and the experience of the passenger, can be pretty horrendous.

Why is this? Our bodies, and to a certain extent our minds, are carefully and fairly rigidly set to a 24-hour clock which keeps pace with the seasons. In any 24 hours there is a series of biological functions that follow a reasonably precise timetable. Jet lag sets this all on its heels, so our body knows not whether it is Arthur or Martha.

Your circadian rhythm—the internal metronome that tells you when to sleep, when to wake, when to work, when to take it easy—is thrown out of kilter because your senses are sending signals that it is light when it should be dark and so on. The body and the brain takes a long time to get over this.

The problems are demonstrated physically, through signs such as heartbeat and temperature. The mental recovery rate is very similar to the physical recovery rate. The problem does not occur if you stay in the same time zone, no matter how far you fly.

What can be done about it? There is, as yet, no sure and certain cure-all. But there are some actions you can take which will act as a form of limited damage control and help you recover quicker.

Work on the general basis that your body needs 24 hours to recover for each two hours of time shift. No time shift, no recovery period. This you may find strange. If you fly London to Johannesburg you suffer no jet lag penalty. But change that to London to New York and you are suddenly in deep strife.

Jet lag affects your judgment. Many companies now have a

rule that business executives may not make a business decision until they have had a full 24-hour rest period. This seems pretty sensible.

My own view is that if I am abstemious with food and drink, if I do some gentle exercise, if I select a flight with the least possible number of stops—preferably just one, Sydney to London—and if I try to remain awake during the daylight hours of my first day, on arrival, I shall be reasonably under control.

Last year I conducted a seminar in Melbourne on a Thursday and Friday, in London on the following Monday and Tuesday and in Amsterdam on that Thursday and Friday. Afterwards I came down with what, at the time, I thought was virulent flu. Now I am quite certain it was my body screaming out for rest.

As I write this I am, yet again, in London. I have just flown in from Thailand on a non-stop flight. I am writing this at three o'clock in the morning because I feel awake and alert. This afternoon I shall get my head down and kip. By thus adjusting my work schedule I will cope with jet lag, but I do not fool myself that I have conquered it.

These are the limited steps you can take to make it easier on yourself.

Keep off the grog while you fly. This may, indeed, be a counsel of perfection, but it is demonstrable that drinking while flying throws an intolerable strain on your ability to adjust.

Exercise. This is not easy. I do yoga every other hour on board the aircraft. On several occasions I have been approached by solicitous flight attendants worried that I was in pain. This worries me not. I would rather look silly than suffer.

When you arrive try not to go to bed; stay awake until night time.

Where possible break your flight. I would never now dream of flying direct Sydney/London unless my nearest and dearest was in severe strife. Instead, I get off at Bangkok or Macau or Singapore or Hong Kong and give my body a chance to recover.

Remember that carbohydrate meals make you sleepy and protein meals keep you awake. Eat accordingly.

Do not take pills of any sort if you can help it. In my experience, and that of most other travellers, it merely postpones and amplifies the agony.

Suntanning

Australians for reasons which are hidden deep within the collective psyche equate suntans with physical and mental health.

A holiday, so the general feeling goes, that produces not a tan is not a holiday at all. It is interesting that reverse applies to nationalities with naturally dark skin. They have the good sense to stay out of the sun's rays.

Yet, because many Australians are descended from Celtic stock, their skins are easily damaged by the sun's rays. Which is why Australia has one of the hightest skin cancer rates in the world.

The Anti-Cancer Council of Victoria has started a campaign with the catchy slogan 'Slip, Slop, Slap'. Which should remind you to slip on a shirt, slop on some suncream and slap on a hat. The effect the sun has on skin depends upon heredity, the length of time of exposure, and the strength of the sun's rays. The quality of sunshine varies from country to country and it is much easier for example, to acquire severe sunburn in Bermuda than it is in Sydney. The reason is that the pollution in the atmosphere effectively acts as a filter. If you are far away from any industrial or commercial zone you will burn faster. What matters is the percentage mix of UVA ultraviolet rays (which are currently considered relatively harmless in moderation but research continues) and UVB which are known to be potentially harmful.

It is worth remembering that sunburn is exactly that—a burning of the skin.

Dr Nearn, a research scientist who specialises in the effect of sun on skin, says 'Tan unprotected today, repent tomorrow'. And tomorrow is not the only time for repentance.

Habitual sunbathing can lead to skin cancer and will almost certainly lead to skin damage of one sort or another. The Chairman of the Health Commission of New South Wales, Dr Roderick McEwin, says; 'Skin cancer is caused by excessive exposure over many years to direct sunlight. The risk of getting it is very high. Fortunately it can be treated. But this should not encourage people to be foolish about their sun-baking habits. The scalp and face, because they are exposed at all times, are most vulnerable to burning and should be covered.'

If you must act like mad dogs and Englishmen and go out in

the noonday sun, then make sure you are protected.

Sun glasses are an absolute must. The stronger the sun, the darker the lenses should be. They not only stop you from squinting into the glare, they protect the tender skin around your eyes from sunburn. A shady hat helps, suntan cream can help even more.

Creams, oils and lotions now have a published protection factor. One is the lowest figure offering the least protection and can only be used on skin that is hardly affected by the sun. Fifteen is the highest and is effectively a total sun block. These protection numbers on suntanning products undoubtedly work.

Simple rules to follow are: if you have a sensitive skin stick to the high numbers; reapply after you go swimming or every two hours; realise that you can get burnt under a cloudy sky; remember that both sea and snow make reflective surfaces which can intensify the rays of the sun, as does water on the body. And consider the healthy alternative of remaining pale and interesting.

If you do get sunburnt there is no way that the damage can be repaired easily. Keep out of the sun, apply calamine lotion or use one of the pain relieving sprays such as 'Solarcaine', take aspirin or one of its derivatives to bring down your temperature and,if it is a bad burn, see a doctor.

Water

Do not drink the water. Forget the assurances given out by all tourist authorities that the water is potable. It almost certainly is—for the locals—but it can possibly contain germs that have no effect on inured local stomachs but may sadly distress yours. Not a slight upset such as we described at the beginning of this article, but a serious infection that can take a long time, sometimes years, to clear up.

The French have the right idea. They never drink anything except bottled water and wine.

Risking the wrath of the Hong Kong Tourist Association, it is worth pointing out that Hong Kong has one of the world's most efficient and sophisticated water purification systems in the world. But in the HKTA office the staff drink bottled water, as does the staff in almost every office in Hong Kong.

When in doubt drink bottled water, soda water or mineral water. Ask for it without ice. If the water is polluted in any way you can be quite certain that the same is true of the ice.

And don't be too sure that if the water is made into tea or coffee that it will be boiled sufficiently—or even boiled at all—to sterilise it properly. In many countries water is not boiled before it is used for making tea. It is merely made hot. The neatest way around this is to carry your own miniature immersion heater—they take no more space than a tube of toothpaste—and make sure that the water is brought to a rolling boil before you make the tea or coffee.

Contact lenses

If you wear contact lenses you have special problems when travelling. I consulted the Sydney specialist Charles McMonnies; 'Always take special precautions when travelling with contact lenses. It is usually best to remove them before you fly. This is especially true if it is going to be a long journey, if you have been wearing them excessively before travelling, or if you intend to sleep on the plane. The pressurised air of the plane has an extremely destructive drying effect on contact lenses, and the circumstances are not ideal for taking them out half-way through the flight.

'Remember to take your contact lens prescription and, if possible a spare pair. Information on the maintenance products used always comes in handy, as the solutions are often sold under different names in different countries. In fact, it is often your best bet to take along enough solution to last you throughout your travels.

'As with many electrical appliances, the heat unit used to sterilise soft contact lenses may have the incorrect voltage for your overseas destination and may require an adaptor.

'When you arrive, restrict your wearing times to allow your contact lens tolerance to be re-established, as jetlag can often cause sore eyes when coupled with excessive contact lens wear.'

Mr McMonnies, as always, gives sound advice.

Flight attendants I know alleviate the drying effect of the atmosphere in the aircraft by spraying their faces with an atomiser of Evian water. This contains pure Evian water under pressure and it comes out in an extremely fine spray. I have found it to work wonders on a long flight and under conditions where contact lenses have started to irritate.

Medical kit

Essentials:

Medication which you are already taking on a regular basis. Plus the prescriptions.

Medication for ailments you get, or believe you get, frequently. Just because I am a hypochondriac doesn't mean I don't get sick.

Contraceptive pills if you use them, because not only is the pill difficult to get hold of, brands are often marketed under different names in different countries.

Paracetamol for headaches, pain and fever.

Motion sickness tablets, if you suffer from it.

Diarrhoea cures. Doctors tend to recommend Lomotil or Imodium. I am not impressed by their performance and would only take these tablets if I were faced with a long journey with limited access to a lavatory. On the other hand, kaolin and morphine works wonders. There is a body of medical opinion that says there are some side effects that are undesirable. This is very possibly true. But if there is a choice between doing my sightseeing from a lavatory seat and running the risk of very minor side effects I will take the kaolin every time.

Tampons can be difficult to come by in third world countries.

Sun cream will help prevent painful sunburn. There is simply no way that anyone can avoid the need for sun cream. In my case I have to use total block out. You should use the level that gives you sufficient protection with a health margin. When in doubt stay covered up. You run the very real risk of sunstroke if you expose large parts of your body to the tropical noonday sun.

Optional:

Iodine.

Calamine lotion for itchy bites, sunburn and minor burns.

Water purifier—either tablets or a filter system. This is unnecessary if you will have access to bottled water or soda water.

Anti-malaria tablets. These are essential if you will be travelling in a high risk area.

Lip balm if travelling in very cold areas or in high altitudes.

Insect repellant cream or jelly.

Antibiotic eye ointment.

Eardrops to prevent infection from swimming.

Anti-fungal cream.

Contact lens solutions. If you wear contact lenses, take a good supply of solutions, they could be difficult to find in certain countries.

Multi-vitamin supplement. If you are travelling for a long time and the food will be sub-standard, multi-vitamins will help to keep you healthy.

The Health Department has a booklet, *Fit to Travel and Return*, which you can get from your travel agent. This gives a good check list and tells you what symptoms to look for when you return.

Finally, anyone who goes abroad, or anywhere in Australia for that matter, and becomes involved in a casual encounter and does not use a condom, is stark, staring bonkers.

20

Travelling with children

A food is not necessarily essential just because your child hates it.
Katherine Whitehorn, *How to Survive Children*

The business of being a child interests a child not at all. Children very rarely play at being other children.
David Holloway, *The Daily Telegraph*

My mother had nine children. I have more than a few. I am experienced in dealing with children—and I am not very good at it.

My eldest daughter, when but a toddler, was left with me while her mother went shopping. I was painting a room and to make sure she did not get her little hands dirty I nailed her nappy to the floor. My wife was not amused. With experience I have improved.

When travelling with children the first essential is to see that they do not get sick. Watch most carefully what they eat. Resist their piteous plea for the boiled lollies and the ice creams. When in doubt give them bottled drinks and packaged food in which you have some faith.

At all times keep them from harm's way. When they go swimming, go along as a life guard. When they explore a town go with them to see they have no accident because of unusual traffic patterns.

Next see that they are not bored. Children do get bored quite easily. You may want to spend the day in Strasbourg cathedral. They do not. Try and look at a potential expedition through their eyes. Remember they are on holiday, not essentially on an educational experience.

When travelling in vehicles the first consideration is to see that they do not vomit. Motion sickness affects children more than it does adults. Give them the anti-motion sickness tablets prescribed by your doctor before the journey starts. Not after the gills have turned green.

Listen to them. Children are much smarter than we think. But do not try to imitate them, emulate them. Getting down to a five year old's level merely makes you into a large five-year-old.

Most of my children are now grown up and I am very proud of they way they have turned out. And we are still a very close and loving family.

My two youngest are Tom, aged 13, and Ben, aged 8. This is what happened when I took them to Florida to see Disney World and Epcot.

It had not been the easiest of journeys. First, Terminal 3 of Heathrow, the anteroom of hell.

We arrive at 9.15 am for a flight due to leave at 11.30 am. I was ever the worry-wart. It takes until 10.55 am to get through passport control. The security is strict, the process interminable. An announcement. 'A blue bag has been left near the check-in counter. Unless it is identified immediately it will be destroyed.' Have a nice holiday.

Pan Am flight 99. I ask for drawing paper, writing paper, pencils, playing cards, something, anything, for my sons. Pan Am does not provide them. But they can watch the movie—*Steel Magnolias*. Not, I think for my eight-year-old. Pass.

Tear up old envelopes and expense accounts and unpublished stories for writing paper. Get going on word games. The cabin service is efficient. Nothing more. Friendliness, enthusiasm, warmth there are not. (On the other hand, on the return trip the cabin crew was friendliness personified. A single bad sector makes not a bad airline.)

At Miami a short wait for immigration. Officer Arroyo has a warm smile for my sons. Welcomes them to Florida. Tells them they will enjoy Disney World and Epcot. Stamps their passports. 'Have a nice holiday.' Means it. Such a lovely man.

I have booked a hire car from Alamo car rentals. Is it not named after a historic, heroic disaster? Perfect for me. Present my papers to a young woman who is bursting with warmth and good health. Big smile, bounteous brown body. Prick her and she will explode fresh Florida orange juice.

She checks my licence and sees it is my birthday. Wishes me a happy one. Presses her warm, firm, brown hand in mine. Because it is my birthday Alamo has a special offer—will upgrade me from a Toyota to a brand spanking new Cadillac Seville which was only delivered last week. I have seen many birthdays. I have grown cynical. I look this gift horse in the mouth. 'How much?'

'Weeeelllll,' she stretches the word into polysyllabic form, 'just $138 extra.' I decline. Reject my birthday gift. She keeps smiling—ah ! the glory of that smile—and battles on.

I have taken CDW which is an extra insurance. But have I thought of the Alamo extra care package which will also cover me for any third party damages in excess of $US200 000? No. Nor did I wish to. The smile stays at 1000 megawatts.

'Well just hope you don't run down any little old ladies. Just two days in hospital and that's your $200 000 gone. Blooey.'

Still, she tells me, it is my birthday and Alamo has selected a special Toyota for me. To my jaundiced eye it looks like the others arranged in serried rows in the parking lot. Drive off with maps and clear directions on how to get to the Florida tollway and then to Orlando. No problems. I keep forgetting that the Americans are the best car drivers in the world. Lane discipline. Courtesy. Not like Australia. Not a hoon in sight.

Off the tollway into downtown Orlando. Well sign-posted as to attractions—Universal City, Wet 'N Wild—but street names are hard to find in the dark. Ask first at a gas station. Get another map and lots of directions. Half an hour later pull into McDonald's and two officers from the Orlando Sheriff's department mark the map.

An hour of sightseeing in the back streets of Orlando and we arrive at the Sonesta Village Hotel. How could we miss? It covers a block almost two kilometres long. Warm welcome. Package waiting from the Orlando Visitors' Bureau.

(It is widely believed that travel editors go around the world drinking vintage champagne from sequined slippers at no expense. Not so. On this trip I bought the air tickets, hired the car, rented the accommodation. No discounts. No freebies. No upgrades. Real money.) The letter welcomes me to Orlando—I had let the PR person in Australia know I was going— and helpfully told me where I could buy all my tickets; that I should start early in the morning to avoid long lines; that I could not be given VIP status because all visitors to Orlando were VIPs (both are true and acceptable); and finished with a list of contact telephone numbers if I needed further information. Fair, friendly and reasonable. It ends, 'Have a nice holiday.' The receptionist beams a Florida smile. 'Have a nice holiday.' All motels should be like the Sonesta. Our unit is a stunning two-storey house. Sleeping accommodation for at least six—more at a pinch. To my sons' delight two extra large television sets. A well-equipped kitchen. And a patio.

The next day Tom and Ben produce their plan of attack. They both go to government schools in Sussex and, astounding this, the majority of their friends have already been to Orlando.

First day is Sea World. An excellent move—it is relatively uncrowded and we do not queue for anything. Once again I am reminded that America is a nation of fat people. We are talking serious fat here.Gargantuan. Tonnes of wobble. Enormous tight tights and straining T-shirts. Not a pretty sight. Every exhibit interspersed with a fast food joint. America grazing. A people on the browse.

Entrance to Sea World costs me $US111.80 for the four of us, about $A150. This seems, as you go in, an outrageous amount. Not so. Worth every cent. Some of the most amazing aquatic sights in the world. My brain goes into overdrive as I see a female attendant soar into the air balanced on the nose of what I think is a beluga whale although Tom says I am wrong.

Tom and Ben stroke stingrays; walk through a shark tank; meet the penguins in the snow; see dolphins spiral up, up, up into the air. We spend most of the day at Sea World, graze on hamburgers, have a spa bath back at the Sonesta.

Dinner at Pizza Hut—gratuities, non-optional, are 15 per cent, says Robin our assistant manager. Only in America has tipping become so formalised. (At the Clipper Lounge in Miami Airport a scotch and two cokes comes to $US4.50. There is a glass full of dollar notes prominently displayed on the bar. It is for tips.)

Later return to Sea World to see Shamu, the orca killer whale, and water skiing with fireworks. My sons call them wicked. This, in the current jargon of the Sussex village, is ultimate approval.

The next day is Memorial Day in America—roughly the equivalent of Anzac Day. We were warned that the crowds would be ferocious. Tom and Ben decide we will recce Disney World—returning later in the week to visit properly. As it happens it is not crowded and we see everything we want to see.

Some observations.

First the cost.

Everything at Disney World appears geared to selling you a five-day passport which includes Disney World, Epcot and some other, minor, attractions. This costs $US135 a head and for a family of four with one boy under nine the cost is a ferocious $US640 plus tax which works out at about $A850. This, on the salary of a working journalist, is a cost that cannot be borne. We worked out that the season ticket is, in fact, a lousy bargain. Better to pay by the day as you go. It still costs $US124.65—about $A165—for four but at least you do not feel you will have wasted tickets if you do not return for every one of those five days.

As my sons will tell you, Disney World can be comprehensively covered in a single day. If you ignore Mickey's Kingdom, which even eight-year-old Ben thought naff, you can travel on every ride, see every show in a single, longish, day. We did.

The queues.

Everywhere we read warnings about the long lines to get into shows. We saw no evidence of this even on a public holiday. The longest wait we encountered was 25 minutes for the Jungle Cruise—and even there the line shuffled along at a brisk pace. (Note most carefully that this is Disney World in Orlando, not Disney Land in Anaheim, California where I understand the queues are brutal.)

Eating and drinking

A small Pepsi—heavy on the ice, light on the Pepsi—costs $US1.25. Four of you sit down for burgers and coke and the bill is $US24. There is, as far as I can ascertain after the most persistent and anxious inquiries, no beer available on the Disney World site.

Silly to recommend any one show or ride. All bloody marvellous. One of the world's great experiences. Like Sea World—expensive but worth it.

Back to the villa through a most impressive thunderstorm.

Next day to Wet'N Wild—a series of inter-linked swimming pools and slides with ride-through tubes called The Black Hole and Hydromania and Kamikaze. Tom and Ben do this for fun. Dear God, I am getting old. Early to bed for tomorrow Epcot looms.

It is too easy a cop out to say that words cannot describe Epcot although there is much truth in this. Think of it physically as a massive figure of eight with a big lake in the top hole. Following advice we start our attack with the top loop covering the national pavilions. This way we beat the crowds. The pavilions are all interesting but China and Mexico and Norway stand out even in such exalted company. We are thrilled and delighted. (Australia does not have a pavilion. Sad. Perhaps it is now too late.)

A quick browse of cheeseburgers and on to the Wonders of Life pavilion where, in Body Wars, we are shrunk in a space craft to microbe size and hurled around the inside of the human body. I am frightened to death and I feel ill, vertiginous and knackered. Tom and Ben love it.

On then to the World of Motion where General Motors has a

multi-million-dollar exhibition which you travel around in a conveyor belt car. Models in this and other exhibitions are called animatronics which means they are, yes, totally lifelike. Elegant humorous touches like pony and trap with a load of chickens on the ground and assorted bystanders giving gratuitous advice. Magic.

Take a break while Tom and Ben swim, then back to the show in the late afternoon and we first see two important pavilions.

From AT&T, the American communications giant, comes Space Station Earth—a title that originally came from Buckminster Fuller who invented the geodesic dome in which the exhibition is housed. I am beside myself with wonder and delight. This show is rivalled, equalled, topped, by that of General Electric called Horizons. And such horizons.

In both of these shows we swim in space, see the vault of heaven stretch to infinity, reach out from spaceship earth and touch the stars. I come away in a state of shock and euphoria. So do Tom and Ben.

Then on to see The Land, educational and calm; Imagination, riotous and funny; The Sea, powerful and moving.

By now it is dark and we buy hoops of glowing, neon-like plastic. Mine is green and I wear it as a halo. So inappropriate. So kitsch. Not out of place. Catches the mood. My sons are not embarrassed.

Down on the lakefront we wait with tens of thousands of others in the warm dark of the Florida night for the last show. It starts with lasers—and such lasers—sweeping across the lake. The pavilions illuminated with a million golden bulbs, hi-fi music. Excitement. Gasps of appreciation.

Now they ignite the fireworks and set the sky ablaze. The show goes on and on—seemingly for ever with crescendo following crescendo. I stand in wonderment until the finale. Then to the roar of the *1812* played fortissimo the sky bursts into light and exploding fireworks and roman candles and flares and rockets and catherine-wheels and fizgigs coruscating, cascading. Lasers lancing the heavens in green and blue and red light and searchlights sweeping backwards and forwards and fountains dancing to the heavens illuminated in colours I have not yet thought of and the roaring cheers of tens of thousands of people. And my two sons beside me in wonder.

Was it all worth it?

By my calculations this whole exercise has cost me the thick end of $9000. Far more than I thought possible. It means my dreams of a new turbo Volvo recede into the distance. My 1978 Volvo will now last me another few years. There will be an ugly scene between myself and my bank manager—not a romantic soul.

None of which matters a jot, I do not begrudge a single cent. If all we had seen had been one of the displays at Epcot it would have been worth it. For my sons and I have seen the glory of the coming of tomorrow. And we saw it as a family. I am content.

21

Romance

I do assure you the climate of Italy affects me much. It inflamed my hot desires, and now it keeps my blood so warm, that I have all day long such spirits as a man has after having taken a cheerful glass.

James Boswell, *letter to John Jonston*

We could not but compare this happy country, Tahiti, to Mahomed's Paradise, where the appetite is never cloyed by being gratified.

George Foster, *A Voyage Around the World*

Put the car away, when life fails,
What's the good of going to Wales?

W. H. Auden, *It's no use raising a Shout*

It is hard for man to make any city worthy of such surroundings as Nature has given Rio.

James Bryce, *South America*

I was ever and always a romantic about travel. My belief is that travel only works if you approach it with romantic anticipation in your heart. Italy is, for me, one of the world's most romantic countries.

Italy

In Italy my nickname is *angelli stronso*—the dirty angel. This odd title was acquired through magazine publishing for reasons connected with my disreputable past which need not be discussed here. The title was given me, as I understand it, by Franco Fasani who is a publisher in Turin and a decent chap. He once drove me in his Alfa Romeo from Turin to Castell del'Mare for a summer sojourn. Like almost all Italians, once he got behind the wheel of a car he became a veritable Signor Toad. From Franco I acquired a love of *la dolce vita*, the very real version of the sweet life that is lived in Italy.

It was from someone else, who was most definitely not Italian, I learned to love Italy in a more spiritual sense. That man was the author H. V. Morton—the initials stand for Henry Vollam. I first met him in 1959 when he was 61 and I was in my twenties. We hit it off right from the beginning. H. V. Morton had started as a journalist on the *Birmingham Post* and had, indeed, been the assistant editor of that newspaper before the First World War.

He was to me then, still is, the prince of travel writers. His writing was from personal experience lightened by research and great erudition. Hear him on the subject of wine in Italy—'I think it is a fairly accurate generalisation that in Italy the wine gets better the further south one goes; it is certainly less adulterated and stronger than the more familiar wines of north and central Italy. Most wine drinkers would give the prize to Castel del Monte, which may be red, white or rosé. Though I think highly of an almost deep red wine called Barletta.' There speaks a civilised man. A man with an opinion but who is quite willing to concede that there are other, acceptable, points of view.

The last time I visited Mr Morton—I never dreamed of calling him Henry nor did he invite such familiarity—was when he was in hospital during the long illness that preceded his death in 1979. He had always been kind enough to look at what I had written and had encouraged me to carry on. Pretty much the last thing I asked him was how I could improve my travel writing. He said, 'Reach out and touch the stones'.

I have, ever since, reached out and touched the stones.

Morton's great love was Italy. His *A Traveller in Southern Italy* was described by *The Times* as 'easily this century's best book' on the subject. He also wrote *A Wanderer in Rome, A Traveller in Italy*. A passionate traveller and an elegant writer.

Thus I gained two views of Italy—almost but not quite one sacred and one profane. This double approach has stayed with me ever since. For while it is true I well earned the sobriquet of *angelli stronso* I also published *Journal of a Soul* by Pope John and visited the Vatican where, because the book had the imprimatur, I had a reader's pass to the Bibliotecha, the Vatican library.

My Italy, then, is an Italy of contradictions. It contains 80 per cent of all the world's great art treasures—a most amazing figure. It also contains a nation that combines Roman, Arabic, Levantine and many other nation's blood into a fiery mixture which is reflected in the conversation, the cuisine, and, yes, the driving.

My guess is that the best introduction to Italy will always be Rome. H. V. Morton preferred the softer south; Sicily is, I promise you, the nearest thing to a semi-tropical paradise that you will ever find. Franco Fasani believed that the world began and ended in his home town of Torino. For me, Rome.

There is not enough time in this life to see all of Rome, to visit all of its grandeur. For this city has been called, with accuracy, the treasure house of Western culture. Summer, the European summer, is not for me the best time to visit Rome. Then it is full of tourist storm troopers taking in the culture of Rome in 18 hours and then off in a lemming rush to other ports. The winter, the later autumn and the early spring are the best times to get the full flavour of Rome. Only then can you reach out and touch the stones and relive the glory that was Rome.

Malaysia

One finds romance where one looks for it. My relationship with Malaysia—Malaya as it was when I was young—has been a long and romantic one.

My maternal grandfather was a liar in the heroic mould. He was also an excellent miner. (Both of these traits are quite common in Wales. I am said to much resemble old grandfather Hughes in some ways.)

Late in his working career my grandfather was working on a tin dredging site in what was then Malaya. He wrote letters home on leaves which were pressed and later kept in the family Bible. Strangely, they never became brittle. The letters were written in Welsh and my mother read them to us with great pride. In Terengganu he said that he had discovered a tribe that lived in huts on stilts. Around the doors of the huts were studded immense fortunes in uncut diamonds—but to remove one was to incur the death wish of the tribe.

He remained poor and I remained gob struck. Diamonds. Tribes in huts on stilts. Terengganu. Malaya. The Far East. For a small boy in Wales this was, indeed, a heady and romantic mixture.

At the beginning of the 1950s I managed to get to Malaya for the first time. It was love at first sight. As I drove over the causeway into Johor Bahru I smelled the magic of Malaya and I was lost, irretrievably lost. The magic of Malaya entered my blood—along with malaria and sundry other ailments—and it has not left. I am a Malaysian incurable and happy with it.

While I was there, on that first journey, I followed up the family story that my grandfather was buried in Kuala Terengganu. Despite the fact that the Emergency was raging, I was able to get there and do a fairly comprehensive search of the public records. There was no sign of my grandfather. This was not surprising as I was later to discover that grandfather Hughes died peaceably in his bed in Rhosesmor in Wales. Lying until the very end.

I last went to Malaysia, as it is now called, two months ago. I came across the border from the Isthmus of Kra, in Thailand, down to Kota Baru. (Sounds romantic but the name means, literally, Newcastle.)

The same old magic had me in its spell; the same smells, the same delightful friendliness of the Malays, the same feeling of a pleasant life in a pleasant land. It was, true, like coming home. I sat at a roadside stall and ate a bowl of laksa and started up my rusty bazaar Malay. It was as if I had never left.

Later, I crossed over to Taiping, that most elegant of towns, where I had spent two years of my youth. Everything was much the same. The water gardens, if anything, prettier. No one remembered me. After nearly 40 years this should not have saddened me as it did.

Malaysia, then, is a green and friendly land and what you will read here is totally biased because I love the place as if it were my homeland. Let us, therefore, get the nasty bits out of the way first.

Malay drivers are lousy. If you hire a car and drive yourself you are taking your life in your hands. I would as lief drive in metro Manila as I would in Malaysia. Leave the driving to someone else.

Pollution has hit Batu Ferringhi in Penang very hard and you are taking a big risk going swimming. Indeed, you will not be swimming, merely going through the motions.

That's it. All the bad points covered. Now the good news. If you have been only to Singapore you have missed the true feeling of being in Asia. In Malaysia they have not pulled down all the buildings in a mad, lemming pursuit of modernity. In Malaysia, the population is allowed to act in a normal and human manner. Public eructations have not been banned as they have in Singapore. The pace is more relaxed, more tropical, more—if you like—Somerset Maugham. (Incidentally, that author is still loathed by anyone who knew him in Asia. He took people's hospitality and used their lives as a basis for his stories. In the British High Commission in Brunei his name has been cut out of the visitor's book with a razor blade. Damn right. Fellow was a bounder.)

To get Malaysia into perspective you need to understand that the country is a long peninsula divided into two sides very different from each other. On the west coast you have most of the major towns. Start at the tip with Johor Baru and then nip up the coast to Melaka. Take a little tack to the right to take in Kuala Lumpur. Ignore the singularly nasty horror of the casino in the Genting Highlands. Move up through the tin-mining town of Ipoh to my lovely Taiping and on to Butterworth. The island of Penang lies just off-shore and is now connected by a bridge.

The east coast is my Malaysia. Start again at Johor Baru and up through Mersing along the coast to Kuala Rompin with Tioman Island over there in the middle of that eye-hurting blue sea. On now along a road skirted with white sand beaches and coconut trees and small kampongs full of smiling, laughing children. Up through Cherating to Kuala Terengganu where my grandfather ought to be buried and along The Beach of Passionate Love (you think I am making this up?) until you come to Kota Baru. Not a major town on the whole trip. Small towns, relaxed way of life, lovely people, scenery that is balm to the soul.

When you go to Malaysia on a holiday (and let us have no ifs about it) you should plan as follows. Two days in Melaka, two in Kuala Lumpur, two in Penang (but do not swim in the sea) and four or five days toddling up the east coast staying at the excellent hostelries run by the Department of Tourism.

Melaka was once—in my time—known as Malacca and it is the most historic town in Malaysia. St Francis Xavier (according to James Joyce, the only saint to get RSI) worked here as did the Dutch, the Portuguese and the Poms. You can see their influences blending in with the Malay Muslim-style of building and the result is a most pleasant town. All the interesting bits are down near the waterfront. Good for buying antiques which may, quite possibly, be old.

Kuala Lumpur is the capital city of Malaysia but it is still an amiable cove of a town. The railway station is a delight, the government offices elegant and the old Selangor Club, the Dog, still a delightfully anachronistic Tudor building in a green setting. (The fact that I was forcibly evicted from those premises diminishes their charms not one bit.)

Penang has its own charms and is subtly different from the rest of Malaysia. There is one hotel in Georgetown called the E and O which stands for Eastern and Oriental. This is a hotel in the traditional style with bedrooms you could hold a dance in. On the other coast the towns are smaller, the charms discreet, the accommodation clean—but not luxurious. This matters not.

Tahiti

Every time I write of Tahiti I find myself using the cliché—Tahiti, *Mon Amour*. But Tahiti is my love. A place that I have returned to more times that I can count. A place to which I shall return again and again.

We had landed at Faaa airport in Tahiti at two o'clock in the morning. The air was warm and heavy with the scents of tropical flowers and fruits. Vahines in pareus had put garlands around our necks. The bus was taking us from the airport to the main town of Papeete. There was a full moon.

On our right was the dark bulk of Tahiti. On our left, the sea—a silver tray in the moonlight. In the centre of the sea, the black high mass that is the island of Moorea. Along the harbour walls were moored the island traders and the yachts. Ahead were the flickering lights of Papeete. The lady behind me tapped me on the shoulder and said: 'Excuse me, if this was the Parramatta Road, would this be about Homebush?'

Thankfully most travellers to Tahiti have a little more romance in their soul. I am at one with Maurice Baring who wrote: 'Tahiti is the whole thing; the real thing; the thing that one has dreamt about all one's life; the thing that made Stevenson leave Europe for ever. All tellers of fairy tales, and all poets from Homer downwards, have always imagined the existence of certain 'Fortunate' islands which were so full of magic and charm that they turned man from his duty and all tasks ... and held him a willing captive.'

Tahiti is, indeed, the Fortunate island. It is so damn beautiful it hurts your eyes. True, Tahiti has changed, is changing. No longer is Quinn's on the waterfront the bar for ramping, stamping, tearing, swearing sailors, French legionnaires and misfits. (Was it not there that a legionnaire, taken with *le cafard*, smacked a wine bottle against the side of my head because, as he later explained, I reminded him of someone he disliked? It was). And LaFayette, the most notorious night spot of the Pacific, no longer runs from late night to dusk with a non-stop demonstration of the hip-snapping tamure—a dance which is, indeed, a vertical expression of a horizontal desire—or features fights on the hour, every hour.

Yes, some of the sweet simplicity of the islands and the vahines is now missing, but this is still Tahiti. The island of Gauguin, of Nordhoff and Hall, of Melville and Somerset Maugham, of Pierre Loti and of, yes, Marlon Brando. A Fortunate isle which is the most romantic spot on earth.

No longer can you clamber on a slow steamer and work your way to Tahiti through a pattern of islands. Instead, fly direct to Papeete, the capital of French Polynesia, with Qantas or UTA or Air New Zealand or Continental. The cheapest way to visit Tahiti—now an affordable resort because the Government forced prices and, anyway, how can you put a price on paradise?—is by package tour. You need a visa. Please note that there is no tipping in Tahiti. Tipping is considered offensive by Tahitian standards and customs and you will look an illiterate boor if you insist. Do not tip. The weather is never less than perfect. The scenery never less than stunning. There are, in theory, two seasons. From April to November it is said to be cooler and drier and from November to March warmer and wetter. I have never noticed this.

In the past I always stayed on the island of Moorea opposite at the Bali Hai simply because of the insanity of the then owners Muk, Jay and Kelly. On the lawn of that splendid hotel I played frisbee with Art Buchwald and James Michener and lost. And then sat with a bucket of banana daiquiris and listened to Shel Silverstein sing mad, bad songs and then danced the tamure through the night. I was younger then.

The Bali Hai Hotel is still there as a sort of condominium. If you stay at the Bali Hai try and get an over-the-water bungalow, well worth the extra money.

The Hotel Hyatt Regency Tahara'a probably is the most upmarket pub and is visually stunning; built on a cliff face. A bus takes you down to the beach for water sports. I also have stayed at the Te Puna Bel Air—which suits me because it has bungalows. The Puunui hotel is on Tahiti Iti the small extension at the end of the island which tourists rarely visit. It has spectacular views and is near the golf course.

To get around there is *le truck* which is unscheduled,

disorganised, impossible to predict but great fun. This is the basic form of transportation on Tahiti and very well may get you to where you are going, eventually. These open-sided trucks start from the market in Papeete. Taxis are ruinously expensive and should be avoided, although they soon will be equipped with meters. Around midnight the prices double. Most hotels provide regular bus shuttles. Hire cars are widely available and are good value.

The French influence in Tahiti is all pervasive. The serious restaurants range from good to very good. Your only problem may be getting a table, especially on Sunday lunchtime when *tout* Tahiti goes out to eat. Wine is a silly price by Australian standards and can range from rotgut to sublime.

Restaurants where I have eaten and which I can recommend are L'Auberge du Pacifique, Acajou in Papeete—there is another in Punaauia I have not tried—and Chez Gerard. The local French population are serious about food and standards generally are high. At some stage try a Tahitian tamaara'a.

What else do I do when I am in Tahiti?

Hire a car and drive around (the road does not go all the way around the island). Go up into the singing mountains. Visit the Gauguin museum. See how accurately he portrayed the beauty of the place and the people. Visit poor Pierre Loti's pool. See the only memorial to a member of a royal family—the Pomare dynasty—that incorporates a bottle of Benedictine. Sit at a sidewalk café in Papeete and watch the passing parade. In ten minutes you will see a dozen of the most beautiful women in the world. Noel Coward did this and hated it. In this, as in much else, he was wrong.

Go out to the lagoonarium—oh, horrid word—at Punaauia and see the fish life of the Pacific. Take the ferry to Moorea—about 45 minutes on the Moorea ferry. While on Moorea go horse back riding on the Rupe Rupe Ranch or ride underwater in an Aqua-submarine and pretend you are a fish.

In 1820, article 23 of the law of the Leeward Islands was passed. It stated clearly that 'all lascivious songs, games or entertainments are strictly forbidden'. A law, thanks be to all the gods, totally ignored. The true nightlife of Tahiti, of Papeete, revolves around the tamure, a dance which has no equal. The Tahitians love music, love to dance, love to celebrate. Papeete reflects this. Especially on a Friday night when the town is wild. There is a tradition in Tahiti that you should wear a flower behind your ear. Wear one and go out on the town.

Wild Wales

I have avoided writing this article for years, avoided writing about Wales. I was born there and left when young. For many years I refused to go back.

Now, some of the old devils have been exorcised so here is my guide to Wales which like Gaul, is divided into three distinct parts. First, there is North Wales which considers itself the only real and true Cymru. The first thing you need to know is that Welsh is a living language still widely spoken in North Wales, especially in Snowdonia. My dad and mam, of course, spoke English but they thought in Welsh and, at home, never spoke to each other in any but Welsh. One of the clearest recollections of my childhood is lying in bed and listening to the grown-ups at supper speaking in the sing song lilt of Welsh. Remember that the Welsh language affects the way the Welsh people speak English. If you ever feel they are being stand-offish it is because they simply cannot understand you.

People who speak Welsh can be extremely, if unintentionally, rude. When an English-speaking person enters an establishment it is standard practice to switch to Welsh. This is because we Welsh have been an oppressed and subject nation for centuries and still act as if we were members of the Welsh equivalent of the maquis—the Taffia.

My dad once stood me outside the ruins of Rhuddlan castle and told me of the two-faced perfidy of the English who tempted the brave Welsh into ambush and then slew the lot. I came away with the distinct impression that this had happened sometime after World War I. It was not until years later that I learned that he was talking about events in the 15th century. The Welsh, the Celts, do not easily forgive a grievance.

Nowadays, far fewer people speak Welsh than is generally believed. Yet it is still the language of the country. Despite desperate attempts by the English in the last century to kill it forever, it survives. All the chapel services I ever attended—and they extend in a Bible black mass beyond infinity—were in

Welsh. So was Sunday school and the Urdd and the Aelwyd and every other society my family belonged to. Hymns were sung, but of course, in Welsh. The names of my family sound strange to uneducated ears—Iorwen, Rhiannon, Buddug, Rheinallt, Meurig, Sian, Ianto Canary, Sion Dafydd. Introductions in my family were ever a spit party.

This Welsh language, despite the paucity of fully fluent native speakers—my guess is well under 10 per cent of the population—dominates the everyday life of Wales. All signs are in both languages. The world's worst television programs (I realise what I am saying and I have given considerable thought to the matter) are shown by mandate in Welsh. To understand Wales is to understand the Welsh. To recognise that we are Celts, that we were oppressed and we have a secret language of our own. That does not mean to say that the Welsh do not welcome visitors. The reverse is true. Let someone in Wales know you are from Australia and you run a severe risk of drowning in tea, suffocating in scones. You will be told, with full and very probably invented detail, about a third generation relation living in Perth. The Welsh believe, totally, in absolute hospitality to the stranger in their midst—as long as that stranger is not English.

In Wales, language goes with religion. The Bible was translated into Welsh in 1588 by Bishop Morgan. My mother's belief always was that it was originally written in Welsh because God is both Welsh and female. Wales has been strongly affected, some would say controlled, by nonconformist religion. The Calvinist Methodists got the strongest grip because all of their missionaries preached in Welsh. John Wesley himself visited several times but Wesleyan Methodism hardly had a look-in because he preached in English. And, by and large, the English are not loved in Wales. This religious influence still is far stronger than is generally imagined. Major strikes—one in a stone quarry lasted three years—were more firmly based on religious differences than on demands over wage and working conditions.

I was born in Caerwys, near Denbigh, which comes from the Welsh meaning no more dragons. Caerwys has much to commend it for it was once a borough, a market town and a seat of the County Assizes. The town received its charter from Henry III in

1290. The first national eisteddfod—literally the sitting down festival—was held in Caerwys under a charter of Elizabeth I in 1568. Upstarts in Cardigan say they held the first Welsh eisteddfod in 1176 with the blessing of Lord Rhys, Prince of Deheubarth. But it was not a national eisteddfod. As far as I am concerned the Caerwys claim is secure. We had the first national eisteddfod but, perhaps, the best national eisteddfod was held in Llangollen in 1858. This is still known as the Thieves' Eisteddfod because the organisers awarded themselves the three major prizes and had it away on their toes with all the takings.

The house where I was born in Caerwys, Henlys, was built in the 17th century and was sold in 1954 for £1250. It has oak floorboards nearly a metre wide.

There are many different ways to arrive in North Wales but the best way is to drive in on the A5 and soar up, up into the singing mountains over the Llandegla moors and then down through the Horseshoe Pass to Llangollen. You will be looking down on the ruins of Valle Crucis as you descend.

Llangollen is a town which I have loved since I attended the international eisteddfod there in 1953 and heard the Oberkirchen children's choir singing its heart out with *The Happy Wanderer* which went on to become a big success around the world. In that year, too, I stood with my brothers Rhys, Meurig and Dafydd on the bridge over the River Dee and sang with some of the great choirs in the world in an impromptu Gymanfa Ganu, a singing meeting, which still remains one of the high spots of my life.

Llangollen is an old town and nearby is Plas Newydd—literally the new place—where lived from 1779 the amazing Ladies of Llangollen. Two eccentric spinsters who held court there for years. They were often mistaken for men. Wordsworth aroused their fury by referring to their stately home as 'a low roofed cott'. Above the town is Castell Dinas Bran whose origin is lost in the mists. I believe that this was where Myfanwy Fychan, the most beautiful lady that Wales ever knew, once held sway.

Llangollen, then, for me, is special. For the visitor it also is special for it is an ideal base for visiting Snowdonia and Anglesey. Everything is within an easy car's drive. A hire car is almost essential for seeing Wales properly. Public transport in the area was never up to much and a car gives you somewhere to shelter when it rains.

There are two glorious sightseeing trips not using the motor car available from Llangollen. The first is in a horse-drawn barge along the Llangollen canal—a branch of the Great Shropshire canal. Before you go on the trip visit the Canal Museum.

The second trip is by train which I will mention in more detail later.

From Llangollen it is but a short drive to Snowdonia. Watch the speed limits. Most of the police in the area are related to my family. Tigers to a man. When I was young I found Snowdon somewhat disappointing. Tryfan is another matter altogether. Stark, forbidding, beguiling, seductive. Often at the same time. This area is the Wild Wales that George Borrow knew. The Wales where Thomas Firbank ran his sheep farm and wrote *I Bought A Mountain*. The Wales of legend.

If you go on from Llangollen to Anglesey, the island that is the mother of Wales, you can visit Llanfairpwllgwyngyllgogerych-wyrndrobwyllllantysiliogogogoch (and I have just typed that without looking it up and, by damn, on checking I see I was right) which was an early publicity stunt that succeeded. Llanfair PG, as it is known locally, had little to recommend it as a tourist destination so in the last century so a local cobbler thought up the name. The longest railway station name in the world came from a fertile Welsh imagination. While you are visiting Llanfair PG to buy the world's longest platform ticket, go and see the Marquess of Anglesey's column which was built by the villagers to celebrate the part he played in the Battle of Waterloo. Climb the 115 steps to the top for a wonderful view of the island and of Snowdonia.

Beddgelert, literally the grave of Gelert, is another example of how publicity can get out of hand. It is almost certain that the story of the brave dog Gelert fighting off a marauding wolf and saving Prince Llywelyn's child was made up by a local landlord in the last century to drum up trade. He built a cairn grave to help the story along. Forgetting that for the moment, Beddgelert is slap bang in the middle of the Snowdonia National Park and is a good place for walking or even making the fairly non-arduous ascent of Snowdon by foot.

Nearer to Llangollen, Betwys-y-Coed has been a touring centre for Snowdonia since the last century. Three valleys meet there—Conwy, Llugwy and Lledr—and the surrounding country is pine forest run by the Forestry Commission which I find somewhat forbidding.

To see these places you can either drive by motor car or take a train—a steam train, a proper train, on one of North Wales's many narrow gauge lines that run in and around Snowdonia. Wales always has had more private railways than other parts of Britain because the full scale railways came to Wales fairly late owing to the difficulties of the terrain. There now are several of the old private narrow gauge railways restored and puffing merrily away. Perhaps the most important of these railways is the Snowdon mountain railway which takes passengers from Llanberis to within a few metres of the summit of Snowdon, the highest mountain in England and Wales. This is technically a rack railway as huge cogs bite into a toothed rail which lies between the tracks. It was opened in 1896 and is still running. The journey takes an hour and, at the end, you have one of the world's great views—if it is not raining.

On the north coast near to Llandudno is the Great Orme railway which carries passengers to the summit of Orme's Head and works with electrically powered cable on precisely the same principle as the trolley cars of San Francisco. This railway was opened in 1902 and lacks somewhat in modern efficiency in that half way up you have to swap trains. What it lacks in efficiency it more than makes up in Edwardian charm.

The best known of the Welsh railways is perhaps the Tal-y-Llyn railway which was originally opened in 1865 and restored by enthusiasts in 1951. It has run continuously ever since. You ride in the oldest passenger coaches in the world still in service. The railway winds its way through Welsh countryside until it ends up at the Tywyn terminus where there is a narrow gauge museum. One that is still being worked on but could become the best train ride in Wales is the West Highland Railway which, in theory, could connect 30-odd kilometres of track from Porthmadog right past South Snowdon to Dinas in Caernavon. The reason why it is taking its time to reopen is that the original railway company is still in receivership.

Llangollen's Great Western Railway station has been splendidly restored from my day and has an exhibition of restored rolling stock and a full-size gauge railway train that, at the moment, only travels three kilometres but may soon go 15 kilometres all the way to Corwen.

Providing you are not there during the international eisteddfod when rooms are literally unprocurable, there are some excellent three-star hotels in the older tradition in the area of Llangollen. The Bryn Howel Country House Hotel is unknown to me but I have stayed at The Hand and the Royal Bridge which are listed as three star and both of which are comfortable rather than flashy.

From Llangollen you can get to the North Wales coast and the carbuncles of Rhyl and Colwyn Bay and Flint. Avoid them like the plague. I once worked in the mills in Flint. The experience haunts me still. You might, if you have time, nip in and see Denbigh where my brother has a pottery in Lon Abraham and then drive through Caerwys where, in the great old house of Henlys I was born.

Head down, instead, by way of Dolwyddelan through Blaenau Ffestiniog with its mountains of slate to Dolgellau. This town lies on the estuary that opens out into Barmouth Bay. Dolgellau, the most Welsh place in Wales. More Welsh, indeed, than Mon, Mab Cymru, Anglesey, the mother of Wales. In Dolgellau the Welsh language lives, triumphant.

This is a town with a great history as three Roman roads met there. It was there, in 1404, that Owain Glyndwr assembled the last Welsh parliament. Gold was, is, mined here. In St Mary's church in Dolgellau is a 14th-century effigy of King Meurig ap Ynyr Fychan after whom my brother was named.

You then only have to cut back towards Welshpool and you are in the heart of Wales, Mid Wales, which is strangely not like Wales at all. It is a sort of wild England. Even the names of some of the towns—Kingswood, Pool Quay, Four Crosses—lack the Welsh flavour.

Mid Wales is the land that everyone forgot. A mystic place. My cousin had a farm there near Pen-y-Gadair. His twin daughters were raging beauties and bright with it. They won eisteddfods all over the place with their recitations. One is now a rocket scientist in Florida.

The border of Mid Wales has a special enchantment. I agree with the poet Houseman who described Clun as 'one of the quietest places under the sun'. All the border towns of Wales, on the wrong or the right side of Offa's Dyke depending on how you look at it, have a discreet charm of their own. On the coast of Mid Wales you come to the unpronounceable Machynlleth which is at the centre of the Dyfi Valley. A fine place from which to explore the wonders of Cader Idris.

In Welsh, Welshpool is Y Trallwng which means, unflattering though it may be, very marshy land. This is because the area is a vast network of pools, Welsh pools at that. Let us leave Welshpool relatively rapidly and head down toward Llanidloes. There you can make up your mind whether to drive towards Aberystwyth on the coast or down through Dolfach to Rhayader and Builth Wells. From there it is but a short hop over the Brecon Beacons to the valleys of South Wales or over to the Gower Peninsula, the little England beyond Wales.

South Wales is very different from the north. It was here that the rapacious English laid waste valley after valley in the search for coal. *How Green Was My Valley* is a pretty accurate description of the Rhondda Valley in those dark days. I lived for a while in Pontypridd which was then a most depressing place. To the left of our house was a pit. Behind us was another pit. To the right was a pit. For a change of pace, in front of the house there was a railway line. These pits took a terrible toll on people's lives. Riding on a bus in Ponty was to listen to a resounding chorus of coughs and spits as silicosis sang its sad song. In my school, the Graig, there was not a boy who had not lost a relative in one of the great pit disasters. All to get coal for England. This has now changed. As our poet laureate sings, 'The pithead bath is a supermarket now'. The tips outside the dark satanic mines are almost covered in green; the River Taff less black. How green, soon, will be my valley. Some things remain unchanged. The male voice choirs, the obsession with Rugby, the intelligence of the conversation.

In travelling around Wales like this you will not, in truth, have travelled far. Wales is not a large country. But in that short compass of time you will have seen Wales.

Wales has many odd corners. Some examples:

You may find it hard to believe but there is surfing in Wales. The coast of Pembrokeshire has become quite popular and Whitesand Bay and Newgate are well spoken of. You can tell the surfers. They are a dull blue colour and their teeth chatter a lot.

Evan James was a great musician in Pontypridd, a town

where music is a mania. In 1856 he and his son James composed *Hen Wlad fy Nhadau (The Land of My Fathers)* which eventually became the national anthem of Wales. There is a statue to them in Ynysangharad Park in their home town. Pontypridd also produced Tom Jones.

The sands of the Pembrokeshire coast are flat and extensive. It was here, on Pendine Sands, that Sir Malcolm Campbell and Welsh driver Parry Thomas broke and re-broke the existing land speed world record back in the twenties. It was here in 1927 that Thomas, a great engineer as well as a world-class driver, lost it while trying to break Campbell's record of 174.88 miles per hour (281 km/h). He was killed.

The Gower peninsula has been 'English' for many centuries. In Norman times this was the Gower Anglicana of the Marcher Lordship. The English who settled there kept apart from the Welsh in Gower Wallicana to the north-east. They still do. I once heard two women discussing another in disparaging terms. 'She's very Welsh.' As if it were a social disease.

The American city of Philadelphia was laid out to the design of the village—now a town—where I was born. This you may find hard to believe. Caerwys was planned in the 13th century in a rectilinear fashion with wide streets. The pattern has since been somewhat spoilt by the inclusion of a roundabout to deal with the rush-hour traffic—my dad's Morris 8, Thomas Anwyl's Austin 7 Ruby and Dai the Milk's horse and trap. Terrible congestion around eight in the morning. Dr Thomas Wynne, who lived there, was a close friend of William Penn and Penn adopted the Caerwys design for the new town of Philadelphia in Pennsylvania.

Prince Dafydd, a true Prince of Wales (difficult to think of the present holder of the title, who is of Greek and German descent, as having anything to do with Wales), lived in Caerwys until he was executed in 1282. A wall of his castle is still there at the back of the old courthouse. This building is almost certainly the oldest lived-in dwelling in Wales.

You will not eat well in Wales. There are one or two excellent restaurants. The rest are not good. My late mother used to make an apple pie which had grey pastry, a teeth-breaking crust and a few acidic apple slices huddled for protection in the middle. My mam had many talents. Cooking was not one of them. This holds generally true throughout Wales. A gourmet's paradise it is not.

(My brother Dafydd has protested over this. He says I have not had recent culinary experience in Wales. That it is full of good restaurants. This is nonsense. Yes, there are something under half a dozen restaurants of international standards. The rest are both dire and dreadful. Wales is the only place in the world where I have sat with a group, ordered the meal and had the waitress burst into tears and explain they have run out of food and been asked to leave and find another establishment).

Dinbych—Denbigh in English—where my brother Rhys lives, is a walled market town with a castle. The town hangs on to the side of a steep mountain and all true residents of Dinbych can be recognised by the size and firmness of their calf muscles. The castle was built for Edward I on the site of an old hall. The main purpose of the castle was to keep the recently-defeated Welsh under the lash. When my mate Emrys was working on the electric wiring in a nearby pub he found a massive well which had a secret passage at the bottom leading to the castle. Until relatively recent times you could see an ancient cockpit in the yard of the Hawk and Buckle inn. This has now been taken to Cardiff. There is still illegal cock-fighting going on in the nearest English county, Cheshire.

Doctor Johnson once visited Dinbych. I have never been able to find anything he wrote about the place. It would have been something rude, I'll be bound.

One of the native sons of Dinbych was Stanley, the man who said, 'Dr Livingstone, I presume'. He ran away from the workhouse in nearby Pant Asaph to go to sea and eventually became a journalist. His original name was not Henry Morton Stanley. It was John Rowlands. He changed it to try to forget his appalling childhood.

Buying souvenirs in Wales is not difficult. Welsh pottery has gone downhill since my family got out of the business but you will still find pieces worth considering. A far better buy are Welsh blankets which are so thick and heavy you can use them as carpets and they will last, I promise you, for ever. At least for five generations.

Food is a problem. The culinary tradition of Wales is not strong. To be truthful, it is non-existent. By and large, food in

Wales is bloody awful, although there are exceptions. Your best bet is to buy Egon Ronay's excellent guides on the subject and follow his recommendations to the letter.

Rio

From Wales I travelled to warmer climes.

When I was young and green, and sang in a choir in a village in Wales, my favourite song told of Rolling down to Rio. The words haunted me then, they stay with me still. 'I've never seen a jaguar, nor yet an armadillo, dilloing in its armour. And I suppose I never will. Unless I go to Rio for these wonders to behold. So rolling, rolling, rolling down to Rio, I'd like to roll to Rio, some day before I die.'

I was so impressed by these words that I went to a library and found a picture of an armadillo in Arthur Mee's *Children's Encyclopedia*. I swore then that I, too, would go to Rio, some day before I died. And by damn I did. Several times. Rio is as wonderful and exotic as the song suggests.

On my first visit to Rio de Janeiro, those oh so many years ago, I was struck by the physical beauty of the place. There are, for me, four great harbours in the world: Hong Kong, Vancouver, Sydney and Rio. Of these, Rio is the most blessed by nature. Everyone who has been there seems to agree.

Charles Darwin wrote in 1836 in his Journal of the Voyage of HMS *Beagle*: 'Following a pathway, I entered a noble forest, and from a height of five or six hundred feet, one of those splendid views was presented, which are so common on this side of Rio. At this elevation, the landscape attains its most brilliant tint; and every form, every shade, so completely surpasses in magnificence all that the European has ever beheld in his own country, that he knows not how to express his feelings. The general effect frequently recalled to my mind: the gayest scenery of the Opera House or the great theatres.'

This view is repeated in writings again and again. Even that dreamy, soap opera poetaster Wordsworth thought 'Rio de Janeiro the best place in the world for a capital city'. And James Bryce, writing in South America in 1912 said: 'It is hard for man to make any city worthy of such surroundings as Nature has given Rio.' Take it as read, then, that Rio is so beautiful it takes your breath away. Accept that Rio is worth visiting for the view alone. There are, however, two sides to every coin.

The crime rate is ferociously high. The best estimate that I can get is that 7 per cent of all visitors get robbed in some way. Not necessarily violent, serious robbery, but robbed, nevertheless. My nephew Nick, who was in Rio photographing for Pan Am, sat on the beach in front of the Meridien Hotel on Copacabana at midday. Standing near him were two policemen. Three desperates from the favelas, the slums of Rio, held him up with knives and took his cameras, wallet and his shoes. The policemen turned away. There is a lot of pickpocketing and handbag snatching in the tourist areas. Dominating the skyline is a statue of Christ on Corcovado, arms outstretched. Under the arms of Christ is a favourite haunt of petty criminals.

When you go to Rio some day before you die, take great care of your valuables. Practise all the standard precautions and avoid showing ostentatious wealth. Do not wear a wrist watch. Do not carry a bag. Use a cheap instant camera. This is especially true during the pre-Lenten period of Carnival when the whole of Rio goes slightly barmy.

To be technical for a moment, Rio de Janeiro—the name means January River—is the chief seaport and former capital of Brazil. Now the capital of Guanabara State, it is a land-locked harbour on the south-west shore of Guanabara Bay. The population is around half a million in the city itself and about the same in the favelas, which have grown in the surrounding hills. The people are an exotic mix of local Indian, African and Portuguese, plus several other minor ingredients. The official language is Portuguese. English is spoken in the tourist areas but is much less common elsewhere. The harbour is dominated, on the one hand, by Sugarloaf Mountain—Pao de Acucar—and, on the other, by Corcovado with its giant statue of Christ.

You can go there pretty much any time of the year because the weather is remarkably consistent and the entertainment is continuous. The hottest months are January, February and March. The coolest are July and August. At its hottest it is like Sydney, at its coolest there is an occasional grey day when the locals all wear sweaters and complain. Carnival is the biggest time of the year when hotels are booked solid. It is a movable feast and runs from the Friday before Lent until Ash Wednesday.

In Rio, hotels range from five star to cheap and cheerful. Prices are roughly on a par with Sydney. All the top hotels are on the waterfronts of Copacabana, Ipanema, Leblon and Sao Conrado. Part of what you pay is for the view. On Copacabana is the Meridien Rio where I have stayed. It is good but sterile. I also have stayed at the Copacabana Palace which I disliked intensely and the Rio Othon Palace which I loved. Out at Ipanema, the Caesar Park is splendid and runs its own security force to take care of guests on the beach.

Driving is no great hassle in Rio and all of the major rental companies are there. The best bet is a locally built Volkswagen Fusca which will cost you about $25 a day plus milage. Taxis are plentiful and about Sydney prices with a couple of exceptions. First there is a surcharge after 10 pm and there is another surcharge for going up really steep hills, such as Corcovado, although many taxi drivers simply refuse to go up. Do not take normal buses. The big, air-conditioned buses called frescoes are fine. Buses do not stop at bus stops unless hailed. Do not use the Santa Teresa Trolley where mugging tourists has become an art form.

Rio lives for its beaches, perpetually disports itself on the 23 beaches which line the city. The Brazilians are health fanatics and wear swimming costumes which make them a scenic attraction in their own right.

If you can, go to the Carnival or, perhaps better, go to the preparations for the Carnival. Rehearsals start in December when the samba schools start working out their routines and costumes. A visit to a samba school, normally situated in a favela, is easy to arrange, though the benches are hard. Brazilians' performance of the samba is everything I was warned against in Sunday school. Once you have experienced the Brazilian samba you will be a changed person.

Rio is the only city in the world where you will see a policeman on point duty abandon his post and samba along with a procession. To get the feel of Rio is to listen to the music of the samba. Not the repackaged, sanitised version of the samba which is played, and played badly, by bands outside Brazil. But the true samba of Brazil. It is, at one and the same time, languorous, sexy, fast paced, impelling, hormone jangling, stirring and strangely exciting. In these properties it is precisely the same as

Rio. For this amazing city is, true, both laid back and vibrant, relaxing and exciting. All at one and the same time.

Take a typical evening in Rio. We start by sitting at a street café facing on to Copacabana beach. The sun is setting but still, on the beach, the cariocas, the people of Rio, are playing volley ball. The women wear tangas—bikinis so small and tight you feel that they must create great discomfort to the wearer's erogenous zone. Brown bodies gleam in the setting sun. Bodies jiggle in all the right places. A most pleasing sight. These women are all, indeed, girls from Ipanema.

We are drinking caipirinha which is a Brazilian drink of great charm and greater potency. It is made by crushing up a lemon in ice, adding some sugar and then topping up the glass with cachaca which is, roughly, Brazil's version of light rum. Two and you are mellow, three and you are nicely-nicely, four and you are legless. We sip slowly.

From time to time street vendors wander around the tables offering us, true, Rio car number plates, lottery tickets, flowers. On the traffic island in the middle of the promenade a vendor has set up a blanket full of leather bags all as cheap as chips. Say $20 each.

There is music in the air and the music is, but of course, the samba. Later, when the sun has gone down, we gather ourselves together and shuffle off with a samba beat to the nearest churrascuria, Mariu's. This is a piss-elegant restaurant with a staff to customer ratio unheard of in Sydney.

We sit in plush comfort and order the standard rodizio menu which roughly translates as all you can eat. To go with it a bottle of Brazilian cabernet sauvignon. This is a little rough but we are a little mellow. The equation balances out. Starters are placed on the table in waves so that plates need to be balanced on the rims of other plates. There are small sausages and tender titbits of beef and eggs and olives and on and on and on. To eat our way through this, the first course, takes an hour. And another bottle of cabernet sauvignon, Chateau Red Ink. The main courses are meat, more meat and yet more meat. They keep bringing it in attack waves until you groaningly beg them to stop. Then a few coffees and on into the night.

Everyone is willing to argue for we all have our favourites. For my money the place to head for is O Viro do Ipiranga which is in Laranjeiras. Here you will hear more music, played better, sung with more soul than anywhere else. We stay until the place starts to close.

Soon, over there, on the horizon the sun starts to rise and we look up and see the statue of Christ the Redeemer on Corcovado mountain looking down with a worried expression on the city of Rio. And there, there, the Sugar Loaf mountain is limned in pink and red and across the bay the islands become visible, one by one. And yes, along the beach, jog and gambol the cariocas of Brazil. All moving to a samba beat.

France

In the gardens of the Tuileries I sat down and wept. Changed. Transmogrified. When I was young I once experimented with LSD. Now, I am ashamed of the incident and would not look at a drug harder than aspirin, and that not often. But in the 60s Leary was preaching his insidious message of turn on, tune in, drop out and I fell from grace and succumbed. In one aspect this experience changed my life for ever. Until that time I had considered all pop music a froth, a nuisance, full of sound and fury, signifying nothing. For me serious music, preferably choral, was the only music worth listening to. Under the influence of LSD, on that first and last occasion, I listened to a group called Deep Purple playing The Book of Taliesin and I was changed, transmogrified. My ears opened.

Ever after I listened carefully to the new music. Some was still dross, some great. My newly expanded senses led me to appreciate the harmonic marvels of The Beach Boys; to revel in the harsh harmonies and harsher lyrics of The Rolling Stones; to take Queen to my heart; to become a devotee of INXS. The Musée d'Orsay in Paris is, for me, a drug similar to LSD. Simple to describe what the Musée is. Difficult to describe its effect. The old railway station of Gare d'Orsay has had the soot and grime scrubbed away to allow its lovely golden lines and decoration to glow and live again.

Inside, the trains have left for their last appointment in Samarra. The platforms have seen their last passenger. Instead is installed an exhibition of art which covers the last 200 years and shows how modern art in all its phases was born. The museum is laid out in a logical order which you should follow. Around the ground floor anti-clockwise then by escalator to the top floor. Again you go round anti-clockwise. Then down to the median floor for a last widdershins circumnavigation.

As you follow this logical order you move from the ornate realism of the early Victorian age to the greatness of the Impressionists and the Post-Impressionists. As you progress a major truth is revealed to you. Almost like Paul of Tarsus on the road to Damascus you realise that modern art in all its forms exists, happened because it was inevitable. No other option existed.

For the curators, the geniuses of the Musée d'Orsay have not just put the best on display although dear God there is enough, and to spare, of that. They have also allowed the mediocre and the appalling to speak. You can see why any artist, any true artist, would have had to react against the restricting, chilling, neo-classicism of the Victorian era.

To walk through an exhibition of those early works is to feel constricted by an artistic straitjacket where slavish realism was everything, imagination nothing. All comes to a climax with a piece of artistic decoration called a medaillier a sort of vertical cupboard which belongs to the Dallas, Texas, Paramatta Road school of art. Quite desperately awful. So appalling that it is, at the same time, highly risible. It is not often that I burst out into loud laughter in an art gallery. The curators, sitting around stern and French on their hard back chairs, took little notice. They appear used to it.

From this, viewed from the right angle, ridiculous nonsense you move through the first groping attempts of the artists of France with a sprinkling from overseas to break the shackles of picky realism. The one artist who holds this exhibition together is Monet who progresses as you progress, whose experiments with light and colour and form show a genius seeking, and finding, a way out of the labyrinth.This is the greatest collection of Monet paintings in the world. Then adding a counterpoint, underlining the changes, the museum has added works of Degas, Renoir, Manet, Toulouse-Lautrec, Van Gogh, Gauguin, Rodin and dozens of others. If, like me, you had believed that Degas was best thought of as an interpreter of ballet dancers and women at their ease, stand in front of the absinthe drinker and feel deep distress at the inevitable misery of her fate.

I had finished the ground floor circuit and was now on the top floor. At about this time, at this place, I felt that I could no longer cope with the emotions, the sensations crowding in on me. I needed a breathing space. The coffee shop on the top floor was open. I sat at a table directly underneath the window that holds the Big Ben-sized clock of the old station. The hands are driven by a small electric motor where I was expecting massy cogs and escapements.

My order was a *bière pression* and a small tuna salad. Then I looked around the room and found my life had changed. For I no longer saw people and tables and chairs. I saw masses of light and dark, splashes of colour, faces that demanded painting, static dynamism. I could see how each scene, each fragment of a scene would appear if painted by a Pissaro, or a Monet or, even, yes even a Van Gogh.

(I have a theory on Van Gogh as I have a theory on almost everything else. If psychoanalysis had been available in his time, and if he lived in New York, the world would have lost his mad, sad genius. For he saw the world with a disturbed eye and that disturbance would have been amended, altered who would dare to say cured? by psychoanalysis.)

I went back into the exhibition and my eyes were assaulted—the wrong word but I can think of no other—by Gauguin's *Joyeuses* which brings back to me, once again, the wonders of Tahiti, my Tahiti.

I looked, with different eyes at more works by Cézanne, by Sisley. I saw, for the first time, the work of artists who up until that time I had been in pig ignorance *La Lotte Bretonne* by Paul Serussier; Emile Bernard who lived from 1868 to 1941 and produced works at the age of 20 which were lyric poems; *La Balon* which Felix Valbotton painted in 1899 and turned perspective upside down. And, as I looked around the gallery I could see as these artists saw. This is not to say I could paint as they painted in that lies their genius. But I could see with their eyes. Before I was blind. Now I could see a reality beyond reality. People are never ugly. They are interesting.

Enough.

In the late spring afternoon I wandered out of the Musée d'Orsay and sat on a bench in the Tuileries outside. I reflected on the greatness of these artists who had changed the way that I saw, the way that the world perceived. This ability to change others is where true greatness lies. Each of these artists, with their clear and unique vision, could change another person's perception. I know my talents as a writer. Dear God, I never claimed to be Ozymandias. My limitations are clear to me although I know, as well, that I am no poetaster. I have a talent, a glib talent. But what I write will never change people's lives. What I write is proficient, well-crafted but never great. Dear Christ, why are the Welsh such a nation of second-raters?

I sat alone in the Tuileries in the early darkness of the Parisian spring evening and thought of the greatness of these artists and how they had now changed my life. I thought of their greatness. And I wept.

Index